NO PLAN B

heart for being
such an essential
part of birthing
this baby.
♡ H

"If you've realized that there is no cure for your desire to be an entrepreneur, Heather has a direct, honest and personal take on how to get from here to there... We each have a chance to make things better by making better things."
— **SETH GODIN, AUTHOR,** *THIS IS MARKETING*

"If you know you want to go for something bigger, but you also don't feel like you're "cut out" for the life of an entrepreneur, Heather Thorkelson is your new salty best friend. She'll give you the straight dope about how you become the kind of person who calls their own shots and does something epic in this world. Less "self help" and more "real talk from a friend," this is the book you need if you're serious about leveling up."
— **SONIA SIMONE, FOUNDING PARTNER OF COPYBLOGGER MEDIA + FOUNDER OF REMARKABLE GROWTH CLUB**

"Heather's book is a lighthouse for anyone who is done living on others' terms and ready to actually work towards getting what they truly want."
— **PAUL JARVIS, AUTHOR,** *COMPANY OF ONE*

"No Plan B was such an easy and enjoyable read. Like sitting down and having a conversation with someone that has a really quirky and fun and relatable sense of humor, that is on my side, that has a decade of experience, and that wants to give me some tough love to succeed."
— AUDREY HOLST, BURNOUT WRANGLER AT FORTITUDE + FLOW

"Omg I love this book! I wish it had existed 4-5 years ago when I was just setting up my solo biz and still felt very trapped by the "corporate mindset." But I also really enjoyed it now, 4+ years into my solo venture — it had me nodding and going "yesss" all the way through. This book is a potential game-changer for anyone who feels trapped in the corporate hamster wheel, as well as those needing a nudge and someone to tell them it's ok to unapologetically bring their whole selves into their business."
— SOLVEIG PETCH, BRAND STRATEGIST + IDENTITY DESIGNER AT PETCHY.CO

ISBN 978-91-519-5692-3

This book is dedicated to
my husband and most ardent supporter,
Rickard. I'm quite certain you had no idea
what you were signing up for when our worlds
collided on that ship in Antarctica. But as it
turns out, your rock solid love and belief in me
is the fuel that makes everything possible.

This is for you if...

You're not just bored, or annoyed, or sick of the 9-to-5. You're fundamentally incompatible with it.

You're ferociously independent, and relentlessly require autonomy and freedom in your life. Subsuming yourself to people's agendas doesn't work for you.

You're ambitious, organized, visionary, and ready to take all the tools available to make work that matters. You know that the only person who can create a big enough sandbox for you to play in is you.

You love to work, get antsy when you're idle, and want to have a bunch of things on the go at once. You have a tendency to take on all the things, because you often can do them — but you need to learn how to best direct your energy.

You want to be judged by the quality of your work, not your ability to play corporate politics, and you want to be valued for your brain, not your output.

You're absolutely on fire to bring your greatest work to the world, and just want to know the very best way to deliver that work. You know there's No Plan B.

Welcome.

IN THE SPRING OF 2007, I found myself walking along an Arctic beach 500 nautical miles from the North Pole.

I was on an expedition to the remote archipelago of Svalbard. (Think: the Swiss Alps dropped in the middle of the Arctic Ocean with some polar bears sprinkled on top.) It was the latest in a series of international trips I took to get a break from my job at a pharmaceutical company...and, to be honest, my day-to-day life.

The company running this particular expedition was owned by Bruce Poon Tip, who I'd known socially for a few years and who happened to join me on the beach that day. As we walked along, we got to talking about my job and how much I hated it.

Bruce asked me what I wanted to do long-term. I told him I always imagined I'd eventually be an entrepreneur, but I didn't know what that would look like. I told him I wanted to do work that mattered, not just filling out spreadsheets that no one would read. Then we both shrugged in that way you do when you both get it, but there ain't much more to say.

I honestly didn't think any more of it, other than to be kind of amused that I'd told an extremely accomplished entrepreneur who'd founded one of the largest and fastest-growing adventure travel companies in the world that I basically wanted to be an entrepreneur when I grew up, even though I was 28 already.

See, back home I had this cushy pharma job that gave me a good salary and benefits including a company car, phone, and laptop. I even got to work from a home-based office, which was pretty much the only way I could have worked in a j.o.b. for any length of time without throwing myself off the nearest bridge.

I had a long-term boyfriend and a freaking awesome dog. I had a pretty rad apartment in one of the best neighbourhoods in Toronto. And I had a lot of autonomy.

But I fucking hated my life in so many ways.

Because here's the thing: just because the optics of a situation are good, it doesn't mean there's not a cancer in the body. My soul was dying, and I didn't know what to do about it.

So, mostly, I drank.

I mean, I "got into wine." It was one part cultivating some low-level wine snobbery and three parts starting to have wine with dinner. Every night. And then top-ups after dinner. And then of course wine before dinner too because you need wine while you're cooking!

I can't even tell you the number of times I almost chopped my fingers off because I was a little bit drunk already while trying to slice the onions. I still cringe at all the near-misses.

But I thought this was all just normal. That's what young professionals in the city do, right? You anesthetize yourself against the day-to-day.

Day in and day out I'd load up my car with samples from my storage locker, drive around to visit doctors who didn't really want me wasting their time, wait in offices for an hour or two until I'd get two minutes to chat with the doc, drop samples, and leave.

Hours of my life that I'd never get back.

Tick tick tick.

Day after day after day.

Driving around the city, waiting in cramped offices, writing reports, coming home, drinking a bottle of wine, and going to sleep in a daze. Waking up only to repeat the cycle.

The thing is, it was always meant to be temporary.

I *knew* I wouldn't survive in that world, but I was biding my time until I got the five years of experience I needed to qualify to apply for a fellowship with the company. The dream of getting that fellowship kept me going day after day, year after year. Sometimes I would go to sleep feeling like I didn't have another day in me. But then I'd remember that I was three and a half years in and only had one and a half more to go until I was eligible. I couldn't give up now!

I also knew that there was no guarantee I'd get the fellowship when the time came, but I needed to try. And I knew that once it was behind me, I was outta there, no freaking question about it. I had zero clue what would come next, but I knew I had to abandon this corporate ship or I'd go down in flames with it.

It took its toll though. Aside from drowning my sorrows in wine every night and justifying it as "the young urbanite lifestyle," I also knew there was something deeply not right with me physiologically. I felt this low-grade toxicity, like my adrenals were burnt out. So I went to the naturopath and asked her if she could give me some herbs or something that would help me feel better. She told me, in the kindest way possible, that I should really think about changing jobs.

I nodded, tears in my eyes, keeping my gaze down so she wouldn't see, because *I knew.* **I knew**...*but...only a year to go now....*

By the time my five years was up, I was literally counting down the days until applications for the next round of fellowships opened.

And I fucking got one.

I was flown into New York for some pre-fellowship training and then sent off to Cape Town, all expenses paid for six months, to lend my professional skill set to an amazing organization combatting the mother-to-child transmission of HIV. It was the most incredible experience made even better by the email I got near the end of my time there saying that one of my company's major medications was coming off patent, and they'd be downsizing dramatically as a result.

I immediately sent an email from South Africa to my manager back in Canada begging her to choose me as one of the staff that would be packaged off. I was leaving either way, but if I could get downsized and have some extra cash to live on, even better.

She came through.

I returned to Toronto in March of 2010, and on June 30th I said a final (gleeful) goodbye to employment. I dropped off my company car at the depot, handed back my laptop and cell phone, and woke up the next day in the unknown.

I truly had no idea what to do next. Zero.

At this point, I hadn't the foggiest idea that starting a business online was a Thing. So after a couple of weeks of just coming down from seven years of employment with the same company, I started to think about what I should do next.

Naturally, since I didn't know the Internet could help me make an income, I looked to alternate career paths. They all looked equally as bleak because they all required me to work for someone else. I knew I didn't want to go back into the same type of situation I'd just left. But I didn't have a skill set I could leverage to work for myself. At 32, I was stuck wondering about my next move and feeling sorely underqualified for pretty much everything.

So I started taking courses in anything and everything that interested me.

I took courses in wine (because of course) all the way up to just before the Sommelier program level.

I worked towards a Diploma in Food Security (which was fascinating and forever changed my world view).

I even took courses in both knitting and sewing. I figured I should use my newfound free time tapping back into my creative side and doing things that were really intriguing to me.

I wasn't sure exactly where I was going, but I knew I needed to figure out who I was and what the hell actually made me happy because, after all those years of dragging myself to work every day and drowning my dissatisfaction in wine at night, I'd dumbed down my sense of who I was.

About halfway through my Food Security diploma, I applied for a master's degree across the country in Natural Disaster Management. Because, you know, helping people and all. That wouldn't feel so shitty, right? Even if I had a boss and reports to write? I could work internationally and problem-solve? Not too awful, maybe?

And I got rejected.

I remember that spring day like it was yesterday. I popped out my front door and grabbed the mail from the box on the porch. The dog sauntered past me and sat at the top of the steps, watching for something to happen on our little tree-lined street. I saw the letter from the uni and opened it excitedly...and then sank onto one of my porch chairs in disbelief. It was a no.

At first I was pissed because I was super overqualified for the program and the rejection didn't make sense to me. And then I was incredibly disappointed. And sad. And then devastated. Because *if not this, then what?* What the fuck was I going to do?

I wasn't afraid or worried, in particular. What I was mostly, was lost.

But that rejection turned out to be a huge gift. I told myself on that porch that I'd give myself 24 hours to feel the feels, and then I just had to get on with it.

And 24 hours later, I felt not only 100% again, but I knew with every fiber of my being that I was never meant to go back to school anyway. Who was I fooling? I hate the structured classroom learning environment! I'm great at learning but absolutely terrible at sitting and listening, and I abhor the classroom and group work. And even worse, the degree program would've only funneled me back to the very environment I was trying to escape: employment.

What the fuck was I thinking?

Of course I'd knocked on that door and tried to go down that road. I truly had no idea what else I would do. I didn't know what else was available to me. I didn't realize that anything else **was** available to me to make a living.

But after the rejection, I didn't really care.

I was done.

From this day forward I would never *wait to be picked again*. I would find a way to carve my own path and figure things out as I went along.

That was the day the true entrepreneur me was really born. Plan A moving forward was self-determination, and there was no Plan B.

I now knew I had to figure out a way to work for myself. But I still had absolutely no idea how to make that happen.

My options, as I saw them, were to:

1. Really lean into the two Etsy shops I'd started as a way to dip my toe into the world of creation and marketing

or

2. Become a Subway franchisee.

(Told you I was still pretty lost at this point.)

I knew I didn't want to run a product-based business forever, and I was batting around ideas for growth capacity. And, because I had no idea what it would actually take to be a "proper entrepreneur," I was also thinking of things like franchising. It seemed like a "safe" route to entrepreneurship for someone who literally had zero experience.

But the more I looked into it, the more I could see that I'd just be trading one prison for another. There had to be a better way.

Then, something pivotal happened.

I discovered that there was something called Life Coaching.

My immediate thought was, "Holy shit, this sounds like some New Age cheese."

My second thought, though, was that getting trained in it would give me some excellent, actionable people skills, and give me experience in running a business, which would be useful no matter what path I ultimately chose. Looking at what was left in my bank account, I enrolled in a yearlong certification program with one of the most established coaching organizations out there, CTI.

Right around the same time, someone I was following in the Etsy community started talking about something called B-School, the now-ubiquitous course run by Marie Forleo that teaches people how to create businesses online. It was weird, but I was starting to see the breadcrumbs appearing before me. The hints and echoes of what I knew I wanted were seeping in through the cracks in my current reality. So I signed up for B-School too.

Truth be told, with both the coaching program and B-School, I loved half of it but being very practical and very non-woo-woo, I took what was useful to me and passed over the rest. I knew I'd be in this for the long game. I knew I had to start building now. And I knew that life coaching was just a skill set, a stepping stone to something bigger down the road.

So, rather than wait until all of my training was done, I put up a website and started taking clients right then and there. I was 100% transparent with people about being in the process of certification. I kept my rates low and my clients' expectations in line with what I could deliver. And I just started building. I learned how to market myself to the people I wanted to serve and I figured out how to get systems in place for my business to run smoothly.

Many of the people in my life coaching certification program were taken aback. Some thought it wasn't right that I was marketing myself as a coach without being certified yet. Some couldn't understand how I was attracting paying clients.

And then I moved to Peru with my partner and dog.

My coaching program classmates were perplexed because they didn't understand how I could possibly get clients if I lived in South America. Was I planning on coaching Peruvians? When I explained to them that I'd be leveraging the Internet to coach clients in other countries via Skype, lots of them were intrigued and wanted to know how they could do the same thing. So I started offering to teach it.

I spent 2012–2015 helping people develop online businesses, and running Adventure Reboot Retreats for entrepreneurs in Iceland and Peru. I also developed The Leap Guide course with Leah Kalamakis (a former client who became an online powerhouse guiding freelancers to freedom), and ran multiple group programs and small masterminds beyond my regular one-on-one work.

Following my own growth as an entrepreneur, I shifted my work to consulting for established small businesses, offering strategy and coaching support to owners hitting new growth phases.

And, while all this was going on, I also founded a polar expedition company, Twin Tracks Expeditions in 2015. Long story short, in 2013 when I was starting to feel the 18-months-into-self-employment burnout I got a call from an acquaintance who offered me a short contract working on an Antarctic expedition ship. I desperately needed a break from my life and floundering relationship in Peru to get a bit of perspective, so off I went.

As fate would have it, I met the man who would eventually become my husband while working on that ship.

By 2015, my serial entrepreneur brain was racing. I was watching my husband and his twin brother working as polar expedition leaders, perpetually on contract with someone. When they weren't working, they weren't making any income.

And yet they were both at the top of their industry: widely loved, in high demand, and physically they're big, strapping Swedish twins, highly recognizable wherever they go! To an incurable entrepreneur like me, it was a no-brainer to take their reputation and excellent salesman skills, marry them with my business-building skills, and create a business that would allow everyone to get off the desperation train of needing that next contract to maintain a living.

Thus, Twin Tracks Expeditions was born. It's a boutique small-ship polar expedition company specializing in transformational travel experiences, serving discerning travelers who aren't really into group travel and have the funds to afford something a little more niche and high-touch. The product we deliver is an exceptional one-of-a-kind experience: taking guests up to the Arctic on 12-passenger vessels to see polar bears, walruses, whales, and all kinds of other Arctic creatures in their most remote, natural habitat.

It's a business that involves a lot of risk and is vastly different from the online ecosystem in which my consultancy runs. With Twin Tracks, we physically take our guests to a part of the world where there's hardly any human presence and options are limited if something goes wrong. But it's risk that's well worth it and the company has grown faster than we expected.

By 2018, I was walking on that same beach in Svalbard that I'd been on with Bruce, but this time with *my* guests traveling with my own polar expedition company. It blew my mind that this is where my entrepreneurial journey had led me. Right back to the very place where I'd first dared breathe the words that I wanted to be an entrepreneur.

I could have never guessed that my path would lead me here. But it's played out that way. And the truth is, when you're an entrepreneur at heart, the "what" doesn't matter so much as the "why" and the "how" — why you're doing the work you're doing, and how much of a chance you take to leverage your skills, creativity, and brilliance.

This goes for you too.

In fact, it's never been easier to act on an entrepreneurial vision. It's never been easier to do the work that truly matters to you, and get paid well for it.

If there's one thing I've learned from all this, it's that even if you start with almost nothing more than an idea, the resources are there for you if you have the vision.

I'm no different from you. I don't have any special advantages beyond any other middle-class white Canadian female. (Granted, being a middle-class white Canadian female is a huge advantage in and of itself. Let's not kid.) But no one has ever assisted me. I don't have an uncle with connections. I've been financially independent since I was 17 and have never had a safety net. I can't move home if things don't work out. I have to bring my ideas to life and continue to build meaningful things that feed me and my bank account.

And you can too.

There is almost zero reason why you can't, other than your own thoughts holding you back.

You have the opportunity to thrive, not just to survive; to be a pioneer in your own little neck of the woods; to do things differently to fit yourself and the life that you want for yourself like a goddamn glove.

You don't need to wait for permission. *You need to choose yourself.*

I repeat: the resources are there.

The technology and systems exist.

The communities of rebel entrepreneurs and freelancers are out here with open arms, waiting to welcome you and help you build your thing.

But to make that happen, you have to understand the full extent of the Matrix that we've been socialized in.

We're so completely surrounded by the version of reality that is the 9-to-5 life. Your friends, your high school mates, your work colleagues, your mom, your dad — they most likely all work within this construct.

It's the *normal* thing to do.

Work all week, get evenings and weekends off and three weeks of vacation per year.

This is deeply, undeniably, fundamentally strange, when considered from the point of view of our capacities as a species.

We didn't evolve to work a five-day 40+ hour week. We're not built specifically for 9-to-5 days. The typical work and lifestyle we live isn't universally mandated by...well, anything. It's an arbitrary series of agreements that most people have gotten on board with. No more than that.

But, when you even hint at the fact that maybe it's not the be all and end all, or that it's not for you, you get a huge reaction.

There's a lot of peer pressure to *not go there*, to not admit that "this doesn't work for me."

And, fair enough, it works for some people. In fact, it works *very well* for some people. That's really great! I'm not trying to convince anyone that they shouldn't like it. And I'm not trying to say that the 9-to-5 is inherently evil.

I'm just saying *let's call it like it is.*

The 9-to-5, the Matrix, this thing, this entity that we have all bought into in the West, isn't the objectively, unquestionably *right* thing to do.

It's not the thing we *should* all do.

It's not the thing we *have to* all do.

So, while I don't have a problem with the concept of working in the 9-to-5 if that's a fit for you, I do have a big problem with the expectation that it's right for everyone, that we're all expected to toe that line.

We're inherently very creative beings. We are not meant to be robots. We are not built, biologically and physiologically, to be automatons.

We know that because the 9-to-5 has led us to be fat, unhealthy, sedentary, and depressed.

There are lots of people, like me, who are screaming to move and create and do something else when we're in an environment like that. And yet we're told that we're difficult or broken. Any suggestion that the system is the real issue gets shot down hard and fast.

Same thing goes for questioning any of the Matrix's core components. Say, for example, that you can only get three weeks of vacation per year. That's the "norm." That's the "standard." That's "acceptable."

In what fucking universe?

On what planet is three weeks of time off per year healthy for a human brain and body?

The fact that we've all drunk that Kool-Aid makes me angry because this system was devised by people who wanted to extract as much work out of us as possible, and your brilliance is so much more than a resource to be extracted!

But because it's been the norm for so long, we don't question it.

Friends, it's high time to fucking question it.

I don't want to be just a vessel of resources to be extracted.

I don't want these old white industrialists to continue to dictate how many days I have to work every year in order to survive.

I don't want the system to dictate that I'm only legally entitled to twelve weeks of (unpaid) maternity leave. What kind of insanity is that?

It's so below baseline it boggles the mind.

And, if you take a second to really think about it, and start to see what life can be like outside the Matrix, things get very interesting very fast.

Because once you're not intellectually beholden to that system anymore, you look back and think, "Three weeks of time off per year? Twelve weeks of (unpaid) maternity leave? Holy shit. I can't unsee that."

Even if you never, ever leave the 9-to-5 system, you at least know what's being done to you. You can demand better. You can advocate for the system to change. But do not let it shape your life. And I mean that literally — how you spend 40 hours a week is how you spend your life.

Whether you stay or don't is genuinely up to you. One choice is not more right than the other – it's only what's right for you.

But if you know that it's time for you to break out (or stay out) of the 9-to-5, this book is for you.

You're at a really interesting place right now. Having become more keenly aware of the Matrix, you now have the unique opportunity to *start asking better questions.*

Just like me after I got my rejection letter, it's time for you to ask, "What *is* next for me?"

It's time to stop asking, "How can I force myself to do XYZ one more day?" and start asking, "What's most important to me?"

"What job wouldn't be too boring and constrictive for me?" becomes "How do I want to spend my days? What type of work and work environment give me energy?"

"What career do I want to have next?" becomes "What impact do I want to have?"

"What box can I fit into given my current qualifications?" becomes "What skill set do I want to leverage to serve the people I want to serve?"

"Who will pick me based on my CV and references?" becomes "Who do I need to become to serve my greater mission?"

"What opportunities are out there for me?" becomes "What opportunities can I create for myself?"

I know, I know...it sounds a bit *unspecific*.

Why won't I just tell you how to be an entrepreneur? Why am I making you think about all these questions?

Because that's the difference between trading one prison for another, and truly doing the work that leverages the best of you to hit that perfect combo of satisfaction and impact.

You see, you have a huge opportunity right here...but you're also at a huge risk point. Because when you've been in the worker mindset for so long, you've been conditioned to think about yourself, your abilities, and your opportunities in a certain way. So many people end up simply trading one box for another — the 9-to-5 system for some imaginary "entrepreneur lifestyle" system, where you do a bunch of stuff that looks good on your Instagram feed and end up flaming out because you've created another job for yourself rather than a business.

I don't want you to trade one box for another, trendy-looking box.

I want you to break out of the box entirely.

This whole thing is so much less about what you're going to *do*, and infinitely more about who you're going to *be*.

You might start out as a freelancer and sell a service that's always in demand, like web design...but it's not really your genius work. It's what you're doing to replace whatever you left, whatever your income was prior to leaving your job.

So the next step beyond just making an income is, "How do I leverage my natural skill set to start building something that matters?"

Like I said, if you'd told me back in 2014 that I'd end up owning a polar expedition company, I would've asked you what you'd been smoking. It would not have occurred to me to do such a thing. The only reason it happened was that I saw a really great opportunity and I saw that the skill set that I had could lend itself well to bringing that opportunity to life. So, we went with it.

Your "what's next" isn't to figure out exactly what you're going to be doing for the foreseeable future. It's getting to know yourself really, really well. You've got to get clear on what your strengths are and then start looking for the opportunities to leverage those strengths in a way that's meaningful to you.

It's all about becoming who you need to become to do what you need to do to create or find opportunities that serve your mission.

It's going to be one of the hardest things you're ever going to do. The stakes though — for you and for the world — make it more than worth it.

Here's the thing: most people crave agency.

They want to feel like they have some kind of control over their future. And in a world that increasingly feels like it's spinning out of control of the average human, being able to ask the questions I mentioned earlier is an act of reclaiming your agency.

Anytime you're dependent on someone else, your personal agency is false, fleeting, and ephemeral at best. It's not *real* because it's dependent on someone else's decision, which can change on a whim, without your input and without all of your efforts accounting for anything.

If you go into any entrepreneurial group and ask, "What do you guys think about working for yourself?" Most people will say, "It's fucking hard man, it's so goddamn hard. Some days I want to scream and throw my laptop out a window. But I wouldn't change it for the world."

Because nobody wants to give that up. Nobody wants to give up that level of agency, that level of freedom, that level of creativity.

When you find the courage to harness your own ideas, to harness your confidence, and go out there creating assets and businesses that matter, that agency is something that *no one can take away from you.*

That is deeply satisfying in and of itself.

And more deeply satisfied human beings are the ones that become empowered to change the fabric of their ecosystems.

When people who were fundamentally created to work outside the system are empowered to go in that direction, we get healthier communities, we come up with creative solutions to problems, we create a kinder economy.

And if you go even bigger picture, harnessing our personal agency means we get the chance to break out of this fucking transactionalist system and stop hurting each other and our planet, and create something cooperative, something better. We save ourselves.

We humans are at our best when we lead by example, because we *learn best* by example. So the more people who are empowered to do what they're called to do and have that freedom to bring their creative ideas to life, the more spillover effect we'll see on the next generation and ultimately, a ripple effect on the world.

Every day you wake up and have a choice.

And once you start to peel back the layers of the Matrix, you can't unsee what you've seen. But you get to decide what you're going to do with that information.

You get to decide whether to carry on within these transactional structures as you were, whether you stay within the confines of these structures but do your damnedest to change what you can, or whether you do the hard work to break free and carve your own path. None of these options are easy and none of them are universally the right option. The only thing that matters is choosing the option that's right for you. And I suspect if you're like me – and the main reason you're reading this book - is that the final option is the only one you can stomach.

This book is for you, dear incurable entrepreneur/self-employed person/ escapee of the Matrix.

But let me be clear: this is not the book where I tell you how to succeed in business. I won't teach you how to get 5000 followers overnight, nor how to jam people into your funnel to get X number of sales this month.

Rather, I will teach you *how to find the answers* you need and, more importantly, *how to ask the right questions.*

We'll also explore how to make decisions about what's right for you and your business when bombarded by 5,000,000 quick-success Internet carrots being dangled in front of your face.

This idea that entrepreneurship is some big, hard, unknowable thing only accessible to people with iron wills and a high risk tolerance is BS. Fundamentally, the act of being an entrepreneur is just a rolling process of finding answers to questions for the thing you are building. Every single day.

It's also really important to understand, especially if you're not connected to the online business world yet, that *you are not alone.*

There's an absolute groundswell of incredible human beings that have been working for themselves online for a good decade, who have leveraged office-based skill sets into other types of cool projects and are doing really well for themselves.

You don't have to reinvent the wheel.

You won't be starting from nothing.
The resources are *there for you.*

This is possible. There's very little stopping you beyond your own lack of self-belief. But please do not fall into the trap of trying to do this alone. You may be a solopreneur, but we all need the village to thrive and we're here for you!

If everything I've said until now is a "Hell yeah!" for you, then welcome to the table.

Pull up a chair.

You're home.

PART 1

WHAT YOU NEED TO KNOW

NO PLAN B **33**

Old World/New World

OK, YOU'RE STANDING IN THE GATEWAY between old you and the new you-know-nothing-Jon-Snow you. The next thing you're probably hoping for is for me to tell you what to do. To unveil my secrets to entrepreneurship and give you the roadmap.

I'm not going to.

See, this isn't another *How to Run a Small Business* guide.

It's not a paint-by-numbers book.

There are no chapters called "How to Replace Your Corporate Income."

I'm not going to teach you how to build a business.

I'm not going to give you any quick tips for success or a sales funnel structure.

This book is also not about me being a coach who's trying to sell you my wares — I'm not trying to manipulate you.

I'm actually trying to scare the shit out of you.

Because the truth is, entrepreneurship is really fucking tough. It is not for anyone who doesn't want it, who doesn't on some level really love it — yes, even during the lowest of the lows.

Look, there are people who work for themselves. People who have billable hours and just deliver their professional skill set outside of a traditional work environment. Call them a freelancer, a solopreneur, a small business owner, whatever. They don't mind doing the minimum viable stuff to market and get clients. They don't mind taking a little bit of risk, and they don't mind when things get a bit hard, as long as there's a light at the end of the tunnel.

Then there are people who are obsessed with turning ideas into things.

Who see an opportunity and jump on it.

Who don't mind taking larger risks for the sake of a really fucking great concept.

They don't mind living in the discomfort.

They don't mind dancing with (seemingly never-ending) uncertainty because they are certain of their own ability to always come out the other side.

These people are as resilient as fuck.

These people are all about imagining what's possible and finding the answers.

They are the entrepreneurs.

Both of these kinds of people need this book, just in different ways. Because both of these types are staring into the face of something that has never existed before.

Whichever type of person you are, *there is no blueprint for what you're creating.*

There are tried-and-true principles that can guide you, but nobody has ever done this thing you're doing.

How do I know this?

Because *they're not you.*

You are here with your own set of skills, your own strengths and weaknesses (both professionally *and* psychologically), and your own invisible barriers of resistance.

Make no mistake, the personal is the tough part. Anyone who's made it through the first few years of building their own thing will tell you entrepreneurship is more of a personal journey...a reckoning...than anything else.

Ernest Shackleton, the polar explorer, famously put up an ad stating the following:

Men wanted for hazardous journey. Low wages, bitter cold, long hours of complete darkness. Safe return doubtful. Honour and recognition in event of success.

This is no different. If we were to sprinkle a little Shackleton dust on a modern-day CTA (call to action) for entrepreneurs, it would perhaps read like this:

Humans wanted to create their own high-risk livelihood. Uncertain income. Intermittent failure and self-doubt guaranteed. Deep sense of satisfaction and a well-lived life in event of success.

I don't know about you, but that last bit fills me with so much hope and motivation that the first bit doesn't faze me.

Yes, it sounds sketchy as hell.

But this book is not for people who aren't up for that kind of challenge. This book is for the people who know deep down that this is the path they are meant for.

The System

Right now, you have an idea of how to succeed. You know of one clear way to learn, be, and achieve — and you got it from the system... the Matrix.

In the system, you follow orders. You've got a job description, deliverables, and deadlines. You try to live up to your boss's expectations and get a good performance review.

You've heard the workplace comment, "This is the way we do things here at XYZ company."

But the thing is, there are so many (often unspoken) rules, so much pressure to conform, and no one is 100% certain of what we're trying to conform to.

Even worse, you're judged on your strengths and weaknesses *in the context* of the system. You're encouraged around your strengths based on *what they want to leverage* from you, and critiqued on your weaknesses in relation to *what they want to extract* from you.

Here's the narrative of how you win in the system: if you kiss enough ass, and get the ear of the right manager, you'll get to the top. As much as we hate it, we've watched the squeakiest, most saccharine, manipulative wheel getting the grease. And that's super hard (and incredibly fucking frustrating) for people with integrity!

Call me pessimistic about office culture, but it sure does feel like everyone is sitting on a throne of lies and judging everyone else. It's not entirely surprising, because the system fosters this. There are a finite number of promotions available. And only the top performers will win the bonus. There's an unspoken undercurrent of dog-eat-dog survivalism because hey, you're not going to work your ass off and not get your piece of the pie, right?

The thing is, there is no pie. You've just been taught to swallow that myth as the One True Reality. (I'll get into this a bit later, but for now, just repeat after me: "There is NO PIE.")

Even worse, you're taught that if you follow the system, if you toe the line, you'll supposedly be taken care of and prosper. Just like Grandpa Jack!

The thing is, dear reader, we're all waking up to understand that this is a whole lotta bullshit.

Here's why:

1. The system is not meant to cultivate and nurture humans. Sure,

there are concessions here and there. But they're the extreme. The system is meant to extract. If that were not the case, then why is legally mandated maternity leave in so much of the so-called "civilized" world so utterly insufficient?

2. You might be loyal to the system (a workplace, a company, a brand) but the system is not loyal to you. To the system, you are a commodity. And you know this.

3. Even if the stars align and you have a lovely professional life without any drama, working your way up to whatever level of seniority and income you like, and retire with a nice pension...well...wait... that doesn't happen anymore! That's an old paradigm! This 1950s narrative no longer reflects our reality.

The system is fucked. There are no two ways about it. And most people are trapped in it. Except for those of us that have a choice. A choice to be brave, to take some risk. A choice to entrepreneur our way forward.

OK so...

BAD NEWS: There is no system for entrepreneurship. There is no roadmap nor clear path to success. There isn't even a clear path to paying your bills!

There is no one telling you what to do next or when to have it done by. So when you suddenly have to wear multiple hats in your work, nothing is clear-cut anymore.

GREAT NEWS: There is no system for entrepreneurship! All that existential dread, that having to play the game, you no longer have to deal with it. Brilliant! No more Janet in accounting. No more having to censor yourself because it's not "professional." No more khaki slacks (unless you actually like khaki slacks). No more filling out spreadsheets that no one will ever read.

And importantly, no more living under the illusion that having a job equals security. When you have a job, you are not the person who decides whether you keep that job. Anyone can downsize you with minimal notice. And to me, when other people or the downturn in the finances of a company can equal me losing my livelihood, that's the opposite of secure.

The even greater news is no one can take your ideas away from you. No one can remove your agency, your resourcefulness, or your ability to generate income from your ideas. That's one hell of a superpower.

So no...there is no system for entrepreneurship.

In place of the system, there's a beautiful landscape of opportunities.

There's the freedom to experiment with creative ideas.

There's the space to figure out where you truly shine as a contributor to others, not just as a worker who does a job.

There's opportunity to reinvent yourself over time, without needing permission or having to quit a job and go back to school.

No, there's no system to guarantee success, but there's an unprecedented amount of resources, of humans that have come before you, and of opportunities to discover yourself and what you're capable of.

Ready to do this then?

Step One: You've gotta unfuck your brain.

Apologies[1] to those of you who weren't aware that your brain is fucked, but it is, son. Fucked in the sense that you've been the repository of a lifetime of conditioning.

It starts the minute we enter school and encounter the rules for proper behaviour: sit, focus, do your work, don't distract other students. Produce, produce, produce. And don't get me started on standardized testing. It's all geared towards forming us into *good workers*, which is the complete opposite of the creative beings that we are born as.

We become creatures that only know how to copy. Hell, I remember being an extremely creative child! I was 100% the dreamy artsy kid of the family. But by art class in 10th grade I'd had the creativity sucked right out of me and I remember feeling distress because the only things I could think to draw or paint or write were modeled on other people's work. That's how young our brains get fucked.

What does this mean for all of us who are fleeing the Matrix?

It means you have to dismantle your internal systems before you can rebuild.

If you don't work through this critical step, you'll likely fail.

I promise you, I'm not being dramatic. I've been in this game for almost a decade as of the first publishing of this book and I assure you — based on what my very own eyeballs have witnessed — that

---

1 I'm Canadian, we apologize for everything!

the high failure rate of early-stage freelancers and entrepreneurs has everything to do with trying to navigate this new world while clinging to old paradigms. *It doesn't work.*

HOW TO UNFUCK YOUR BRAIN

The key is to get away from the pull to conform. The drive to search for formulas and structure outside yourself. To look for quick fixes or to copy what others are doing as a shortcut to success. This does not work.

(Aside: there's a massive difference between *copying a business formula* and building a business *based on tried + true principles that's still unique to you*. I'll get into that later.)

The starting point of actively deprogramming your brain is to leverage your "weaknesses," as perceived by the system. Yeah baby, get back to the exact stuff that's been ripped from your marvelous human synaptic-magic hands.

This non-exhaustive list includes:

Creativity

As a general rule, creativity and offering outside-the-box solutions are not welcome inside the Matrix. We've all put forward a great idea to a boss who said thanks-but-no-thanks. But outside the Matrix, creativity is a muthafreaking superpower extraordinaire. Everything that is awesome in the world was birthed from a creative mind. Time to leave the black-and-white behind. We're in kaleidoscope-land now.

Noticing opportunities

Same as above, noticing opportunities and gaps that can be filled is often pooh-poohed in the Matrix. I've never seen so much resistance to following a thread of opportunity or filling in a problem area than I did when I worked for companies back in my 20s and early 30s. I always wanted to yell, "Why won't you just let me make this better?!"

Outside the Matrix? FUCKING SUPERPOWER. Noticing opportunities is everything. Noticing opportunities and unusual synchronicities is why I have a flourishing polar expedition company. Noticing opportunities is why Apple products exist. Do not underestimate this. They tried to take this skill away from you — "It's too risky!" "Nobody likes someone who thinks they know better!" — and you are going to goddamn well take it back, sister.

Testing theories

Again, general rule: inside the Matrix, they don't want you messing around with different ideas and theories. They want the shortest line from A to B. Productivity and profit, baby! If there's an established way, you're expected to follow it. We're not used to the idea that "this might not work" — which, by the way, should be your new mantra, forever and ever amen. (Thanks Seth Godin!) But I'll come back to that. We're not in any way primed to try different things and indeed, it gives most people anxiety: 95% of people cringe at the idea of split testing their email newsletter headline. "Can't I just use one thing that works?" Sorry, Alan, but no. You must test. You must become comfortable with exploration again.

Looking at data that doesn't directly correlate to an ROI

This is a big one, because the traditional world is focused on productivity and profit. But out here in the creative human-centered sandbox, the nuanced data matters. Out here, we need to examine context more than anything. It's no longer enough to just look at the "hard" data of list numbers and conversion rates. We have to be able to collect, parse, and use the data related to "soft", human things. Empathy, psychology, buying behavior, the sheer complexity of the humans involved. Understanding these? That's what wins this game.

Understanding humans as 3-D in-living-color beings, not cash piñatas

The irrational factors of human behaviour, the unpredictability, the soft round edges...those insightful details matter. Inside the Matrix, everything needs to be categorized to work — people have their job description, and their function, and their deliverables. There's little room – and little tolerance — for complexity. Outside the Matrix, that complex, "problematic" behavior is just...human behavior. And knowing how to roll with that is a superpower.

Perso-fuckin'-ality

I'm about to be Captain Obvious here, but it bears repeating because it takes a long time to really get this: having personality is not about mimicking the successful people in the room, it's about being yourself.

And, being yourself does not mean mostly cloning a successful person's website and then tweaking it to make it more "you." Everyone sees through that shit and exactly no one is inspired by it.

But here's the thing: being yourself is actually pretty hard when your brain is still numbed from the system. I know I sound like some kind of ranting revolutionary, but it's just the truth. It took me almost a year to get back to myself after I left the working world, and I thought of myself as a creative person with a pretty healthy level of self-awareness!

We — all of us — get dumbed down by the system. We do! We're more malleable than we realize. Yet it doesn't mean that we can't rise from the goddamn ashes of conformity like the motherlovin' redwoods that we are with our ancient DNA and scrappy, steadfast resilience.

Enter the terror.

"Ok....shit, what now?"

I get it. It can be a little overwhelming to see your full set of new world resources for the first time. And it's normal to feel unprepared...to feel like who you're supposed to be in this next phase is still a bit out of your reach.

That's OK. You haven't been this self yet.

It's like someone becoming a new mother. She doesn't know who she is in this identity yet. Yes, the baby is new, but so is her mother! She's never been a mother before, and it happens in the blink of an eye. That's a crazy identity shift to navigate.

The same deal goes for you. You don't know who you are as an entrepreneur. You're discovering yourself in this new identity. We like to think we know ourselves sooo well, but holy god if I had a dime for every self-employed person I know who's been on the bathroom floor crying because of all the internal shit that entrepreneurship brings up, I'd be Oprah-rich.

Here's the deal: you don't need someone to tell you WHAT to do. There are a million courses and websites out there you can draw upon as resources to find the technical answers you need.

Rather, you need to know HOW TO THINK about who you are

and what you're trying to do. That's what this book is about. We're no longer down with other people's agendas, we're only focusing on yours.

In other words, there's no right way to do this process, but there are smart ways to think about it.

And that's why you need to know about the entrepreneurial cycle.

The entrepreneurial cycle

I know the majority of people reading this book will be the type who list "want to help people" in their list of business whys. I'm one of them too. But as much as the altruism feels nice, we've gotta start by looking inward first. Because you and I are in this for the long run, and that means we need to build sustainably. And everything sustainable must start with the needs of the self and emanate from there.

To keep carrying on the mom/baby metaphor I mentioned in the last section, the baby will best thrive when the mom's needs are truly met. And hey, your business is your baby! Even if you're a dude...you're a dude who's having a baby! Congrats.

With that in mind, all human-centered business exists in the same iterative cycle, answering these three questions:

Who am I?
What do I want?
What am I going to do about that?

No matter what you do, as long as you're among the unemployable, your process will play out according to these three questions. You'll continuously deepen into them over time, getting more and more solid on 1 and 2, which opens up ever more options for 3.

The answer to "Who am I?" slowly reveals itself as you unfuck your brain and you get back to what makes you tick, to what energizes you. It becomes clearer as you get more honest, peeling back the shoulds and, especially, shedding other people's expectations of you. (OOOF!! Fu-cking HARD, that one.)

The answer to "What do I want?" is the next stage, and on the surface, it seems to be more clear-cut: "I want more freedom! More money! More time to do the things I like!" Right?

It's actually much more nuanced than that, because you have to figure out what those things actually *mean*.

What does freedom mean to you? What does more money look like? What would it take for you to feel successful, like you've arrived? This takes an incredible amount of introspection, of trial and error (because you're still figuring out who you are), and of realizing new truths that you weren't expecting.

The answer to "What am I going to do about that?" is the part that will most directly inform your choice of business model at any given time. Gone are the days of set-it-and-forget-it business. You will evolve, and your business will change. And that's a good thing! It takes the pressure off getting it right the first time. Get it to good enough, and then fine-tune until you're ready for the next evolution.

You're going to change significantly over time, so you'll need to come back to these three core elements over and over and over again. Who you are as a decision-maker in your business right now is going to be different from who you are five years down the road. You evolve and your business evolves, depending on how deeply you sink into these core questions.

Let's delve deeper into each of them.

Who am I?

Captain Obvious here again: understanding who you are in your core is pretty much a baseline for doing work that matters. It comes first, because nothing else will fall into place quite right unless you're clear on this piece.

And look, I know you're self-aware. Like me, you feel fairly clear on who you are. You've got well-informed opinions, and you know who you are in relation to others.

But we need to get more granular. We need to get into the nuances of what makes you tick. You know how all the mega-successful people talk about things like meditation and having a life coach as keys to their success? It's because they know the nuances of self is where the gold truly is. They don't push it away simply because knowing oneself doesn't have a direct ROI. They dedicate time and money to it because it's mission critical for entrepreneurs.

All deeper knowledge starts with asking questions, right? So let's run through a few top-line Qs to get you started.

An important reminder: Answer these questions as freely as possible, without the lens of judgment. Don't worry about whether your answers sound selfish or carry some other negative connotation. Getting to the truth here is more important than social norms or how you want to be perceived. And anyway, these answers are for your eyes only. So be really, really honest.

1) What gives you energy?

Give this some serious examination. What work environment has given you the most energy? What tasks do you truly enjoy? What environment feels amazing for you to exist in when you need the creative juices to be flowing? What rhythm during the day allows you to feel most healthy, both physically/mentally and in relation to the work that you do? How do you identify on the introvert/extrovert scale?

This last bit is especially important because a lot of us don't examine the introvert/extrovert paradigm until we're out of the Matrix. I didn't understand that I was an extroverted super-introvert until I was 32! While I'm a hyper-social hand-talker that can find something in common with just about anyone when I need to, my preference is near-hermitude, and I'm happier than a clam when I can be alone (like, for a week) and not have to talk to anyone. This directly affects how I designed and run my businesses. Because it has to. Or my businesses won't work.

2) What drains you?

Equally important is getting really honest about what sucks your energy out. What do you find incredibly boring or pointless? What is the epitome of tedium for you? What makes you feel like you'd rather poke your eyes out? What type of people do you find it insufferable to be around? What elements of a work environment throw a wrench in your creative wheel? Be honest! Write down unpopular thoughts.

Here are a few examples: I HATE meetings. Truly hate them. And I can't stand people who drone on forever, wasting time. I also get very drained by being around people or having to work with people who aren't efficient or make excuses all the time. I feel super deflated and held back from my own genius when I have to contend with these. So I created a business ecosystem where I don't have to.

3) What are your values? What forms your inner compass?

This isn't something that gets a lot of air time. If you've never done this before, you may find it difficult because we imagine ourselves as good people who value everything! But I'm going to ask you to pick just five. Five core values. That's the hard bit — narrowing it down!

How do you know which five form your inner compass? Make a list of all of your strongly held values and then go through and ask yourself, "If this value *isn't* honored, would I be OK with that?"

In other words, your core values are the values you cannot live without. You cannot tolerate it when they are overstepped. And that's cool. That's great, in fact. Now we're getting closer to the true you.

Kick off your list with inspiration from the list below, or google "core values" and see which ones stand out to you.

Accountability	Family
Adaptability	Freedom
Bravery	Generosity
Commitment	Loyalty
Communication	Professionalism
Creativity	Recognition
Curiosity	Respect
Decisiveness	Service
Dependability	Sustainability
Equality	Transparency

4) What are your (higher self) pet peeves?

I added "higher self" because it's easy to answer this with things like, "People open-mouth chewing," and that's not what we're looking for here. What we're looking for are pet peeves that are an extension of your values. Examples might be: poor customer service, people who don't take personal responsibility, customers who don't pay on time, chronic lateness, etc. Think about the things that really drive you bananas when you encounter them in *any* area of your life and then free-write a list. You'd be surprised at how much this will inform your business decisions moving forward.

5) Who do you want to be?

I can feel you staring blankly at me right now. "Uhhhh...I don't know, Heather, who **do** I want to be?"

And I know...I get it...I've been there. How are you even supposed to answer a huge question like that? Some people are tempted to just say the most outlandish thing they can think of. For instance, one client once told me he wanted to be "the next Oprah." But shooting high isn't the point. Running *your* business as *your* highest version of *you* is. And a nebulous answer is OK, because it all helps point you in the right direction.

I suggest narrowing down your answer with these two prompts: Imagine yourself 10 years from now. What would you in 10 years want to look back and see?

And, 10 years from now, how do you want the people around you (employees, friends/peers, family, clients/customers) to feel as a result of how you show up? How do you want them to describe your influence on their life?

What do I want?

Answering "What do I want?" is important because it helps you break free of old thought patterns, getting clearer on what makes you you and peeling away the old paradigms of what you thought was possible for yourself.

Think about it: When you were entrenched in the Matrix, what did you want? To become a manager? To make enough money to buy a Tesla? To retire early? To be respected by your colleagues? To earn more vacation time per year?

"What do I want?" comes second because you need the "Who am I?" answers as a baseline to move on to these questions:

1) What do you want in your life?

More what? Less what? What have you been yearning for? What do you never feel like you have the time for? What do you spend too much time on? What brings you the greatest joy in work, and in play?

2) What impact do you want to have? What's your bigger picture?

Related to the exercise above where I had you look 10 years ahead, what is that bigger-picture impact you'd like to have? You might not know the answer to this yet. And don't feel like it has to be some huge goal.

Answering with, "I'd like to know that I helped a handful of people I adore keep their online communities running like a brilliantly well-oiled machine" is just as valid as "I want to look back and know I helped thousands become financially literate in their business" or "My contribution was letting expats know they were not alone in their challenges through the work I've done." Big or small, your impact matters.

3) What do you want your days/weeks/months to feel like and look like?

This is hugely important! It's a critical element of business planning, because the main thing you want to avoid is creating a beast that you're not interested in managing a couple of years down the line. It's long-game planning.

It's the reason I never started a Facebook group when literally everyone had one (and was making money from it). I didn't want to be a slave to something that wasn't enjoyable or interesting for me to engage in. So please do spend some time thinking about what you want your days, weeks, and months to look and feel like. You can reverse engineer how your business is set up to honor that. And you can thank me later.

4) How much freedom and flexibility do you need?

Think about this in terms of where you currently wish you could show up more. It's likely tied in with honoring your core values more closely. Have you had to miss your kid's sports games in the past and really want that to change? (Hint: this impacts the structure of your offers.)

Do you need to be able to work from anywhere? (Hint: this impacts business design.)

Be really honest about what you need in terms of freedom and flexibility. And if you write down that you're gunning for a #TimFerriss four-hour work week, please throw this book down immediately and run away. (How did you get this far!?)

5) How do you want to show up for yourself? For others?

Our egos want us to answer the second part first. Or maybe it's the inner people-pleaser, depending on who you are. So I encourage you to think about how you want to show up for yourself *first and foremost*. Once you've got that down, think about how you want to show up for others, but remove the ego bit as much as possible. Death to the "I want to be a thought leader" nonsense! This is not about how other people will perceive your proverbial greatness. This is about how you make other people feel. And not at the expense of your own well-being. See how the order of these two matters?

6) What have you been missing professionally?

This answer might be similar to some of your answers above, and that's OK because we're not just mining for truths, we're looking for patterns. What have you longed for in your work or your work environment? What frustrated you? What did you feel like you had no control over that maybe now you could control in this new world order you have in front of you?

What am I going to do about it?

Friend, this final question *is* your way forward. You've examined who you are in this space and time, you've explored what you truly want, and now it's time to put the pieces in place.

This is your jumping-off point, and the rest of this book is going to help you figure out how to do this. Again, we're not approaching this from a tactical perspective. Tactics are free on the Internet. Instead, we're coming at it from the personal, deep-rooted place of how you build something that is synchronous with who you are and who you want to become. This is about legacy work, even if you're "just a web designer." (And FYI, no one is "just an XYZ" in my opinion.) This book is about changing our ecosystems through entrepreneurship.

And it's all part of the iterative cycle.

The whole point isn't to reach an endpoint.

You'll come back to the iterative cycle over and over and over and over again as you change and grow and become — and as your business changes and grows and becomes — because it will mean different things each time.

Being an entrepreneur is less about the form that your business takes and much more about who you become — because that's the single most important factor in your ability to achieve the success or reach that you want.

But first, we have to talk about risk.

Risk and Failure

I KNOW, I KNOW. It was all going along so well. You and me and the rest of the incurables...set to take on the world! Why bring in unpleasant subjects like risk and failure? Taking risks and (gasp!) failing are the worst parts of this whole self-employment thing, right?

They are the *parts that shall remain unspoken.*

They're the subjects that our parents warn us about when we dare hint we might try this start-a-business thing.

But friend, we have no choice. We're obliged to go into those seemingly dark spaces because believe me, you don't want to trade in a job for another type of cage. And, if you don't learn to redefine your relationship with risk and failure, you'll end up doing just that.

Without a healthy grasp on these two inevitables, you'll stay small. You'll stay in a space that you've convinced yourself is safe, when in fact it's just limiting. You'll continue trading dollars for hours which, let's face it, ain't much better than working for The Man.

Being an entrepreneur is about evolving into an ever-bigger comfort zone. You're going to need both the hard and soft skills that allow you to be in a good relationship with failure and risk, so you can have the confidence to move through your own resistance to reach the next level of your work.

Bear with me here, because it's not as painful as you think. In fact, I'll show you how to be as zen as can be about failure and risk.

What is risk, really?

We've all gotten the mini lecture at some point from one of our older dude-friends that goes something like, "Lemme tell you something about fear. Our fear instinct once kicked in when there was a real threat to life and limb...like a lion descending upon us for his dinner back in hunter-gatherer days. But these days there's no real threat to life and limb, and yet we feel terror over things that are nothing more than our own thoughts. Our living/habitat circumstances have evolved but our emotional responses haven't."

Or the self-help favourite: "F.E.A.R. is just False Expectations Appearing Real. So you really have nothing to worry about!"

The thing is, it's all true.

We were built to have a physiological response to stress that would allow us to stay alive. And here we are in the modern day, facing down situations that can't possibly kill us, and yet we're paralyzed by fear and therefore unable to dance with any real modicum of risk (or *perceived risk*, which is a whole different layer).

In other words, our modern perception of risk is highly unbalanced.

Researchers have found that the purpose of fear and anxiety is to signal your body that a threat or conflict is coming up, and trigger it to respond accordingly. This means that fear is actually a motivational state. It's your body's way of prepping for defense or escape.[2]

Read that again: "defense or escape." If every time we feel anxious about something we run away, we'll never do anything worthwhile! In fact, that's why most people don't follow even the tiniest of their dreams. But then again, we're not most people.

It doesn't help that the societal narrative about risk helps shape our soft little kid brains and we then grow up with a skewed concept of what we should avoid. When I was growing up, I was taught by both my parents and the dominant social narrative that being an entrepreneur or an artist was extremely risky, and that only irresponsible people or those with a trust fund would choose that route. I was told there was a high failure rate and that what I really needed was a good white-collar job and the good manners to make sure I was well-liked and therefore safe.

Lemme tell ya, the good manners part of all that was the only true bit. And not even the well-liked part. That part is way overrated.

Which leads me to the modern-day social media–soaked version of our reality where we now think it's risky to post a photo of ourselves that maybe isn't perfect. Or to launch a website/podcast/anything because — oh dear — someone might have an opinion that isn't 100% positive.

I hate to state the obvious, but that's not real risk. If the potential

---

2 If you want to nerd out on this, check out https://www.ncbi.nlm.nih.gov/pmc/articles/PMC3181681/

outcome of you taking a risk is that you feel bad, you don't have a risk issue, you have a perception issue.

In the context of this conversation around stepping into the entrepreneurial decision-maker you need to be, **a risk is a thoughtful, bold action in service of achieving a better result.** A risk is something that, if it doesn't work out, results in acceptable losses.

Risks vs. gambles

Let's contextualize risk even more, because I *really* need you to get comfortable with this in order to move forward. The next layer of risk aversion that society piles on us is that risk is something *irresponsible*. Only the rebels, the immature, and the thoughtless take risks. Nobody tells you that a risk is a good idea when you're about to take it.

But after the risk...oh, after! That's a different story. You take a risk for love, or a risk for glory, and everyone sings your praises when it works out well. You feel me here?

Pre-risk-taking, human observers are a nervous herd of sheep bleating the same warning. Post-risk, they are your biggest champions as they throw you up on their shoulders and expound the virtues of your brave soul.

Friend, do not let the bleating of the sheep sway you.

Rather, learn the skills of discernment needed to identify a *risk worth taking*. I'm going to help you here with a simple differentiation between a risk worth taking and a gamble.

Both a risk and a gamble involve taking a bold action that has a chance of success.

With a risk, if you lose, you can accept the consequences and recover. It might hurt and you might walk away with some bruises to your ego and/or some damage to your cash flow, but you can recover. The consequences of failure aren't terminal.

With a gamble, though, losing means you have to face unacceptable consequences. If you lose a gamble, you're not just hurting, you're out of the game for good. You're not embarrassed or cash-poor, you're out of business. And what's even worse about gambles is that when you lose, you tend to double down on your original course of action, assuming that if you try a little bit harder, want it a little bit more, then you can pull yourself out of this slump. (This is actually a formal logic thing called the gambler's fallacy.) The stakes are too high and you can't afford to give up, so you pour more and more of yourself into this gamble, only to have it bite you in the ass again and again.

So, to recap: A risk is a bold action with possible consequences you can accept and recover from. A gamble is a bold action with possible consequences you can't accept or recover from, and that will only get worse with more action. And, above all, our perception of what's "safe" is just a societal narrative we've bought into.

With me so far? Great! Now that we have a common understanding of risk, you can start redefining your relationship with it, which is essential for making it as an entrepreneur.

The Two Stages of Fear as an Entrepreneur

Stage 1: Fear of Incapability

OK, so we're not living in 1989 anymore. Being an entrepreneur doesn't seem as wild and crazy as it once did because hey, there are lifestyle entrepreneurs all over Facebook so it can't be that hard, right?

Nevertheless, it all seems very "unsafe" when you're still in the early stages for one reason and one reason alone: being an entrepreneur does not come with a steady paycheck.

And let's be honest: most people define safety as financial security. And it's true, there is no guarantee of financial security in entrepreneurship. (Upside? No one can take your job away when you work for yourself.)

But that's not what this fear is ultimately about. What's really underneath this fear of financial insecurity is the fear that you are incapable, that you don't have what it takes, that you don't know what you need to know and don't know where to start, and even if you did, who's to say that you can actually command the prices for your services or products that will allow you to replace your former salary or — gasp — live well?

If you're wondering how I'm able to pull that information so accurately out of your brain, it's because *everybody* goes through this. Most people in the early stages of business have a website that's kind of crappy, have clunky systems in place, and feel like a fraud a lot of the time. It's not fun, and you'll often question your capability and whether you deserve to be at the proverbial table at all.

I'm no exception. I had a *totally* shitty website when I first launched it in 2011. I was in one of the first rounds of Marie Forleo's B-School and I was surrounded by a community of new entrepreneurs who seemed to have a shit-ton more money than me (which wasn't hard, because I had approximately no money) to invest in websites and professional photo shoots.

Me? I learned basic web design and built my own site with my own novice graphics, and my old bandmate Satpal took some photos of me for dirt cheap because he was happy to do something a little different from his primary gig of photographing Indian weddings.

My whole entrepreneurial existence looked like amateur hour, and while I believed in myself (albeit precariously) I wondered if anyone else would believe in me. I wondered if anyone else would think I was capable and actually want to pay me money to help them. I was so painfully aware that I didn't know what I didn't know. How could I learn what I needed to know to grow a healthy business and convince people to pay me at the same time because hey, I had a mortgage to pay!

But I stayed the course because for me, there was no going back. And here's what I can tell you for sure:

You are capable. You can do this.

Loads of people with less smarts or resources and more responsibilities (kids, mortgages, whatever) have done it before.

As much as we like to fool ourselves, these "successful people" don't have a magical superpower or some secret insider knowledge imparted to them at a $10k-to-attend special midnight mastermind with Shawn Schmedley, the 7-Figure Guru™. The people who have come before you have used the same resources and gone through the same growth stages as everyone else *because that's how business works*. It's a skill set, a knowledge set, and a mindset, not a secret.

Look, whenever you feel doubt about your capability, just look around on the Internet at your so-called competitors and see how many of them are just peddling the same old shit. Same message, similar websites, you name it. Some people aren't even that charismatic or original, yet they're making bank.

Honey, if they can do it then so can you. Full stop.

And for the record, many of those people from my entrepreneurial community back in 2011 — the ones with the kick-ass websites and perfect photo shoots that I was intimidated by — have closed up shop and gone back to being employed. The moral: don't compare other people's business outsides with your entrepreneurial inside.

There is nothing stopping you but you.

"But, but, but Heather...am I too late? Hasn't the Internet bubble burst? Aren't people over being shoved into someone's sales funnel? Don't people have online course exhaustion? Aren't people's NLP web copy–detection ears on high alert these days? Isn't it super hard to list-build now?"

Nope. On the contrary, this is still the beginning.

Things have changed, sure. Consumers are smarter, absolutely. The get-rich-quick phase of Internet marketing is phasing out. *And that's a good thing.*

(#sorrynotsorry Tim Ferriss, but your *4-Hour Work Week* created a hot mess of people with unrealistic expectations and, consequently, broken dreams.)

Underneath this breakdown of the dude-bro approach to treating the Internet like a cash machine is a fundamental shift in the way the digital world interacts. The BBC *Business Insider* program interviewed me about this stuff back in 2016, and some old stuffy British man asked me if digital location-independent businesses were just a fad *even back then*. It was radio, so he couldn't see the eyeroll that almost broke my face, but suffice it to say I told him the same thing I'm telling you now: The Internet is not going away. Work is diversifying and will only continue to do so. This is the future. If you can provide value, you can do this.

You have nothing to lose.

When you have a job, you have something to lose. A job is something that another person or a corporate decision can take away from you. There are a million reasons your job could cease to exist overnight, leaving you with highly specialized knowledge you'll never be able to use again.

But in working for yourself, you reclaim agency over both your work and your life. Yes, it's tough. Yes, it's uncertain. But the genius of working for yourself is that as long as you have a brain and a pulse, you can deliver.

My husband once said to me not long after we met that he worried about my income security if something were to happen to me physically. And I was all, "Look, even if I became paralysed from the neck down, I can still do what I do. All I need is my brain and the ability to communicate to generate an income. Everything else is logistics, and it's figureoutable."

So start where you are.

Start with *something you can do*. You're not going to be Brené Brown right out of the gate. You might have a very in-demand and easily marketable skill set, which is great! You're ahead of the game! But if not, just do something. Anything. An incurable entrepreneur can't afford to be snobby about how they make a living in the early days. Start with chickens in your backyard and sell their eggs if you need to. (I'm not even joking here.)

Whatever it is, find a way to provide value.

From there, you'll find other ways to provide value, until eventually you find *your* thing, and then you can iterate that in any number of ways forever. When I left my j.o.b., I opened up an Etsy shop selling stuff I made just to dip my toes in the waters of marketing and selling. That led me down a path of breadcrumbs to a coaching certification, and the next evolution of my self-employment became life coaching.

But life coaching and my wee Etsy shop didn't pay the bills, so I took a course on web design and started building budget websites for people in my online business community who needed a basic website to get up and running. These different, but adjacent, paths allowed me to learn how to run a business with the skills I had at hand. They started teaching me *who I was* as an entrepreneur.

My life coaching practice became a business strategy practice because my life coaching and website clients, as it turns out, were mostly people who needed to learn how to run their businesses. And since mine had been on the upswing for a couple of years, during which time I moved from Canada to Peru, I had valuable insight to offer.

By 2015, I'd opened a polar expedition company and my business-strategy company naturally matured into its next phase of supporting established entrepreneurs from all walks of life and business models.

Here's the thing: in the process of starting *wherever you are*, you learn *who you are*. We don't hatch out of an egg knowing who we are as entrepreneurs. No matter how self-aware you fancy yourself, you learn a whole different spectrum of information about yourself when you step onto the entrepreneurial conveyor belt.

And you can't skip this stage. I know, I know. But it's true. Remember what I said earlier about deprogramming your brain from everything you've been socialized to think and feel towards work, risk, personal value in the workforce, etc.? It takes time. It also takes time to find out what your real strengths and weaknesses are in the context of self-employment.

The nice part is that if you're willing to lean into the journey and *show up* with curiosity and humility, you'll naturally evolve into who you need to be.

The old refrains of "I'm not good at XYZ and I can't do ABC" become "I don't know how to do XYZ but I can figure it out. I'm weak in ABC, but I'm going to improve."

While it sounds gentle, most seasoned entrepreneurs will tell you this evolution is like a spiritual bitch slap to the face. You go through a ton of self-development during this process because you're not just staying in your hidey-hole anymore. To ship this dream of yours, you'll constantly be called to scary places, and the thing is, *you want to go*. It's worth the pain of growth because the pain of things staying the same has become too much.

So, to recap: stage one of redefining your relationship with risk is understanding and accepting that you *are* capable. What's possible for everyone else is possible for you. It's time to take your place at the table, and decide to reframe this whole thing as an experiment. And your only job is to start *where* you are so you can learn *who* you are.

Stage 2: The Fear of Capability

Allllright...now that we both agree you're capable, the next hurdle pops up before you young Padawan: "What if I can do it, but it's/I'm not good enough?"

Hooray! Just what we need. A whole new type of mindfuck!

If I had a penny for everyone I've ever worked with who got super hung up on their website being "perfect" before it launches, I could've retired on my dream alpaca farm with my electric car parked out front back in 2014.

Look, we all want to look like we have our shit together. We think no one will hire us or buy our services/products until we look like we've "arrived," until we are visibly successful, whatever that means to you. We might be comfortable with our value, but we want our outward presence to *prove* that value for us. We want testimonials and logos of companies we've consulted for or whose podcast we've been on. We want kick-ass photos where we look 15 pounds lighter than we actually are.

Because the reality is that the most prevalent, visible examples that new business owners notice are successful, "perfect" entrepreneurs who have their shit together. So we think we have to look like that from day one.

But you know what that is? This desire-for-perfection-out-of-the-gate thing? *It's because you're still trying to fit into the corporate model of value.*

In the corporate world, you're valuable when you fit a certain box. You know this. You've felt the injustice of undeserving people getting kudos because they're more flash than others. Because they say the right things, look the right way, or kiss the right arse.

And you know what? *Fuck that.* I'm going to repeat what I've said before: you didn't escape the working world just to live in a similarly shaped box. We have the opportunity to redefine what value looks like, and it doesn't have to be flash. It can be subtle.

In fact, true story: a number of the most financially successful and well-loved entrepreneurs I know and follow are the opposite of flash. They're plain Jane. Some of them don't even have a photo of themselves on their website. Some of them haven't updated their site since I first stumbled upon them in 2011. I kid you not! And yet, these folks are wildly financially successful and well-loved for their work.

When we get stuck in the corporate model of value, the one which values outward appearances more than anything, we're stuck in nothing more than a giant procrastination wheel. It's the "I can't do X until I get Y just right" stuff.

Please, I beg of you, work hard to let this go! We are waiting for you to deliver your skills and your passion. We are waiting for your help, your insight, and your service. Don't let old paradigms *keep you from showing up*. Show up in spite of them.

Marianne Williamson famously stated, "Our deepest fear is not that we are inadequate. Our deepest fear is that we are powerful beyond measure. It is our light, not our darkness, that frightens us most."

There's a reason everyone loves that quote so much: we know it's true. It's like an uncomfortable gut-punch of feels. The corporate model of value, the polished "perfection," has to go if you want to do work that matters.

For now, focus on good enough. I'm talking minimum viable presence needed to get your work into the world.

And then show us how good you are. Through your actions, through showing up, through connection, through adding real value.

A shiny Internet presence doesn't mean fuck-all if there's Swiss cheese behind it. I mean, look at my earlier example. Of all those people with the fancy shiny websites who took B-School with me in 2011, only a *small percentage* are still in business.

Success comes from practicing your craft, not imitating what looks like others' success on the Internet. Go listen to Guy Raz's *How I Built This* podcast and hear the real stories of founders and relatable visionaries who were eating rice and beans for three years before they got traction.

And ditch your old ideas of what an entrepreneur is, or does, or looks like.

An entrepreneur is not someone who has built a specific, successful business. It's someone with the skills and knowledge to build any business with any opportunity they choose to work with.

And how do you actually embrace that? By changing your relationship with risk and failure. "OK, great Heather. Let me get right on that," I hear you say. Well, it's easier than you think. You just have to understand this:

Failure isn't real.

People think failure is a reflection of them and their value, and that it is final and devastating. Once you've fucked up, that's it. You had your chance, you blew it, and now you're going to be exposed as "a failure," not someone who has failed at something. It becomes an issue of identity. They also often think that failure is their fault, when a lot of times what's seen as "failure" in the Matrix is actually just the system doing what it does, and your human bits getting caught in the middle of that.

The truth is, a failure is just when something didn't turn out the way you expected. Simple as that. But we're taught to attach so much *value* to it. Just think about how these sentences make you feel: "You failed. The launch failed. Your business failed." They make you feel horrible, right? But the truth is, they're just statements of fact.

As da Vinci proclaimed,

"Experience is never at fault; it is only your judgment that is in error in promising itself such results from experience as are not caused by our experiments."

That's why I always advocate for taking a more scientific approach when it comes to risk and failure.

I approach things with the mindset that whatever happens, however you "fail," it's not a bad thing. It just didn't turn out the way you planned. The upside to this is when something didn't go as planned, you now have data to work with. You can ask yourself, "What happened? Why didn't it work? What can I do differently next time? In hindsight, what was missing this time?" This gives you so much great data to work with and to inform your next phase of development!

And, this is exactly why you start small. You start where you're at, where your failures won't kill you. In fact, most of your "failures" won't even register with anyone other than you.

So if failure isn't *a thing*, if you take away its power, then what you're actually doing is a series of experiments. You're testing ideas. You're gathering data. You're seeing who you are, how you want to put yourself out there, and what sticks when you do. A big part of your job as you deepen into your entrepreneurial self is to learn how to look at the data neutrally.

Because look, you're not dumb. You're not going to make decisions or take actions that aren't supported by data and some degree of experience. Your job as a business owner is to dually be able to take risks and also minimize risk.

Take the example of our first season operating in the Arctic. I put deposits down on two separate charter dates — one in June and one in September — on a really nice ship. These deposits were 20% down on a ship that cost tens of thousands of Euros to charter. The June trip started selling immediately and we were fortunate to have a group of travelers take up half the ship.

The September trip was taking longer to fill, but bookings started to trickle in and we had two really fantastic pro photographers as guides for that trip. When the date came for the second deposit to be made on the September trip, we only had four bookings out of 12 and nine months left to fill the ship. I was pretty confident that we had the network and reputation to pull it off, even though we were new. And on the other hand, I knew it was entirely possible that we *couldn't* pull it off. Eight sales of a $10,000 product is no small feat for a company in their very first year with no marketing budget. So I asked myself just before I placed the second deposit, "If we have to cancel, and I lose the equivalent of a year's college tuition in some countries, will I be OK with that?"

This wasn't company money. This was my own personal savings from the sale of my home in Canada and it was a big percentage of it. The risk was real, with personal implications for me.

As fate would have it, after I'd made the second deposit some of the four folks already booked on that trip had a falling out and decided to cancel. That left us with one booking, seven months out. I made the agonizing decision to pull the plug and take the financial loss. It was a real-life kick-me-in-the-bank-account-balls moment, but the upside is that I learned a lot about the marketing/network/sales process when it comes to higher-end travelers and, even better, I'll never make a misstep like that again. Of course, I had no way of anticipating that we'd have cancellations like that and had we not, I do believe we would have pulled the trip off. So I don't think it was an error in risk assessment per se. But since losing that investment, I've become *much* more active in generating market awareness of our brand and product.

That "failure" directly informed my choices in strategically growing the business for year two. And I'm happy to say that we went from two expeditions (we ended up picking up a second expedition later that year) in our first season to three in our second, and four in our third, which is a solid amount of growth for a niche market. In the end, the risk was what it was, and the loss was tangible, but the reward of greater knowledge and developing my entrepreneurial aptitude cannot be underestimated.

So if failure isn't real, and everything that happens is just information, suddenly, risk becomes a lot less scary. Because here's the thing: when you redefine your relationship with failure, your value is no longer tied to the whims of anything external.

Your value is no longer on the table.

In a job, your identity is inextricably tied to that job, and your value is on the table. This is true whether we like it or not because it's how society defines us. "My mom, the nurse. My sister, the geologist." If Mom does a bad job being a nurse, it's a direct reflection on her value as a contributor to the system. Ugh! That doesn't feel nice!

I've always felt very strongly that who I am is not my job title. I had an entrepreneur's soul long before I started my first business. My mom used to proudly introduce me as "my daughter Heather, the pharma rep" and I'd be screaming inside! First off because that's not how I defined myself (I saw myself as a musician), and also because I was ashamed of working for big pharma. I didn't need it blasted out at dinner parties.

But my mom, bless her heart, was just proud of me. She was proud because in her eyes I'd succeeded in the Matrix, and that was just the best thing a parent could hope for. Security! Status! Value in the corporate world!

Or as I like to call it, assets and titles that can arbitrarily be taken away from you in the blink of an eye. Aka: Bullshit. Empty. Nada.

I don't know where it came from but for as long as I can remember, I've been brutally aware of the fact that no matter how loyal you are to a company, the company is not loyal to you. Yes, there are a few exceptions, but they're rare. Knowing that to a company I'm a vessel from which resources should be extracted does not make me feel valued at all. I think that's why I was always somewhere on the spectrum of depression when I was employed.

But as an entrepreneur, your value is up to you. Titles and positions only matter in the system. Outside of it, you are you. And while this is kind of terrifying to some people, it's fucking fantastic once you get into the swing of being a label-less maestro of bringing creative ideas to life.

No longer are you tied to your skills. Just being your creative, ineffable, curious self — sans job title — is a superpower. Like I said earlier, your value isn't on the table when you create your own livelihood. You're no longer a cog! You're a creative scientist. You're an imaginationfueler. You've moved from peering out of the Matrix asking, "What's possible?" to standing boldly outside of it saying, "What's *not* possible?"

In entrepreneur world, your value isn't on the table because it's not tied to one position or function. It's also not tied to failures or work volume production. As an entrepreneur, you survive *and grow* by leaning into the things that didn't work.

That's why it's so critical that you start out the journey by taking stock of your hard and soft skill sets, learning where your weaknesses are, and then going and micro-failing in those areas so you can learn, recalibrate, and then get better. Then you "fail" bigger, recalibrate, and get better, etc. etc.

Above all, you have to remember that even on your worst day, *you* don't suck. You're doing the best you can with the tools and knowledge that you have, which is not only fantastic but brave. The fact that you're taking a chance, that you're dancing with risk for the promise of something better, of something more worthwhile, is more courageous than the 99% that would never go there.

Truly embracing the fact that failure isn't a thing, and that your personal worth is not inextricably tied to the ups and downs of your business, will completely shift your relationship with uncertainty, which is the other big thing that throws off new entrepreneurs.

Getting OK with uncertainty

OK, so we've redefined risk, and you're starting to get the picture that your value is no longer tied to anything external, and, therefore, nothing can actually hurt you. Sounds absolutely fantastic in theory...but what about all the little uncertainties of day-to-day life as an entrepreneur?

This is where the rubber really meets the road, my friend — because while you can be absolutely on board with the idea that failures are just experiments, when you're down in the middle of something, the uncertainty of not knowing how it's going to turn out (and maybe not even knowing what you're going to do tomorrow!) can drive you crazy.

If you're going to make it as an entrepreneur, you have to get OK with big-picture risk as well as the unnerving hum of constant, low-level uncertainty.

This is one of those inalienable, fundamental, baked-into-your-soul kind of attributes that every entrepreneur must have. It's a non-negotiable for doing work that matters.

Why? Because it's constant and inescapable. (Yayyyy...)

No matter how much data you have, there's never a guarantee your idea will work. Never ever ever. We *all* know of examples in life where something seemed like it would be an obvious success...a real shoo-in. Like opening up a Subway sandwich shop across from a high school kind of no-brainer. But the biggest illusion we suffer from as humans is that we have control. That we can predict with a good amount of accuracy what's going to happen. And we're so fucking wrong, so much of the time! Especially when we're breaking new ground. So, repeat after me: no matter how much data you have, there's never a guarantee that it will work.

This is actually a great thing, for a couple of reasons. Being in active relationship with uncertainty keeps you on your toes, iterating, improving. This is the most genius bit of the dance with uncertainty. And despite what your immediate reaction might be, staying on your toes doesn't need to be stressful. As soon as we start to rest on our laurels, the world catches up with us and blasts past. Who wants that?

Not me. I want to be the one who's always looking for the bit that's been overlooked by most people. I want to find the opportunity that others haven't noticed and go there. Knowing that it's all uncertain anyway gives me free rein to try something different. To innovate with reckless abandon.

Uncertainty reminds you to remain forever flexible. It reminds you of the importance of staying curious, of not being lazy about things. The unavoidability of uncertainty is also proof positive that there's no such thing as a set-it-and-forget-it business. If that's what you're gunning for, any success you experience will be short-lived because people change and market behaviours evolve. What works now probably won't work as well a year from now. In fact, I guarantee it won't work as well a year from now. I don't know about you but when I worked in a job, the predictability of it bored me to tears. While a lot of people would shy away from work that requires constant evolution (of self, of your business model), many of us *crave* that. This *does not mean* that your profitability will be unpredictable or uncertain. It means that the way you serve your customers will be flexible enough to rise to new occasions and in fact become more valuable in both directions.

Because when you can approach everything with a "this might not work" attitude, your whole life gets freed up. And I really mean this. You know what they say — expectation is the mother of all disappointment. So when you take the approach of "this might not work" to everything you do, there's no fall from grace. There's no rock bottom of disappointment, followed by the self-flagellation of "I suck, I failed." This leaves room to celebrate the success when it does work, and remain relatively unsentimental when it doesn't work, looking at the data/conditions that led to either result. And then, you can think of next steps: What now? What's the follow-up plan? How can the data inform us to try things differently next time?

This is a fundamentally more powerful position to act from, because it means you never get stuck. Uncertainty is what keeps most people in inaction. So many people are paralyzed by not knowing the outcome (which is impossible anyway!), and therefore they don't have the confidence to take action. You know it's true. You've been there. We all have. "I don't know what will happen so I won't take the risk." Think of the people who you know and love that you wish would have done something — applied for the school, asked for the date, moved abroad for a summer, started that business — because you know it could have potentially transformed their life.

Uncertainty is the dream killer. It's one of the most self-limiting beliefs that no one talks about. And it'll keep you in inaction unless you decide you're not going to let it.

So many people struggle with uncertainty because it's a deeply uncomfortable emotion. But I'll say it again: no matter how badly you fail, you will almost certainly not die or end up living in a box on the corner. So you don't need to fear this emotion as deeply as you have been. Instead, practice holding it in one hand, while holding your wisdom/self-belief in the other.

You are much more capable than you give yourself credit for, and that's not some New Age platitude. There's no reason creatives can't teach themselves to approach things in a more scientific way, asking things like "Why am I feeling this way? Is the risk I perceive real or imagined? What does the data I have tell me? Why am I doubting myself — is it legit or just a bad thought-habit I fall into when the stakes feel high? Are the stakes really that high? What is the worst possible outcome of this scenario and would I be OK if that happened?"

Finding uncertainty deeply uncomfortable isn't a reason to try to avoid it altogether. It's often a signal that something greater awaits you on the other side.

And if that's not motivation enough for you, remember...uncertainty is the dream killer.

And I mean this on a very personal level. With these past two decades of gurus telling us to find ourselves and find our passion, most of us have been left adrift. I believe the "find your passion" mantra is deeply flawed because it ties our happiness to a specific thing...this elusive "passion."

The reality is that there are only a handful of people who have a true, wild, deep passion that they can make a career out of. It's the "I've known I wanted to be a baker since I was a little boy" people.

And lemme tell ya, I'm not one of those. And I'd venture to guess that most creative entrepreneurs fall into my camp. The idea of having a passion feels so limiting to me. I have lots of passions! I'm passionate about customer service and turning ideas into real things, and amazing yarn, and good manners, and cheese, and facilitating transformative experiences, and snail mail, and alpacas.

Being uncertain of what you want to do day in and day out is a really tough place to be. I know because I spent a lot of time there...over a year, in fact, after I left my corporate job and watched my savings dwindle month over month while I sat there in the park with my dog wondering, "What the fuck? What now?" But then I picked one thing. One thing that I knew would be a useful skill to build.

And from there, other opportunities and ideas opened up. In short, I spent the next few years learning how to become an entrepreneur. As it turns out, I haven't built two businesses because I found my passion. I've built two great businesses because I figured out what kind of work energized me and how I best serve others with my strongest natural skill set. The rest of my entrepreneurial skills are learned and/or a work in progress to support my core work.

That's a lot of mindset shifting...but the good news is, the better your relationship to failure is, the better your relationship with uncertainty will be. Because uncertainty is a lot less scary and disconcerting when you know you can't fail...when you know in your bones that you'll keep figuring things out, in spite of any setbacks, and keep growing into the person you're meant to be, creating the legacy you've longed for.

I'm not going to lie to you: it's going to be hard. One of the hardest things you've ever had to do, in the heart sense more than in the head sense. Because it's going to require you to get over yourself.

The beauty of getting over yourself.

Is this the hardest part of being an entrepreneur? Probably. Likely. But hot damn is it worth it. Because the absolute unflinching truth is that the main blockage between what you have and what you want is in between your own ears. Yes, there may be institutional barriers and external elements at play, but how you manage your own damn self is controllable, and that's what we need to focus on.

That's why you have to get over yourself. And you know what? Everything you could possibly need to grow and evolve is available in spades, often for free. We've never lived in a time when it was so easy to access the tools and info needed to do stuff outside of conventional norms. Never! And yet we still shy away from the opportunities before us because no one has set out the no-fail breadcrumbs for us to follow.

So, I need you to wake up every morning — like I {try to} do — and get over your bullshit. From the niggly things, like getting up on time and putting your ass in the chair to do the work, to the big existential torments of "Am I good enough/can I do it?"

On the inside, this looks like getting control of the self-doubt, procrastination, and resistance that pops up in your brain. And I don't mean "getting control" as a one-and-done scenario. I mean get control of it as a habit, as a practice. Because honey, these three mofos are going to be your new Golden Girls. Always bloody there in the next room and always with something to say.

You know that whole narrative that you have to overcome incredible odds to be a success story or to earn credibility? What they don't tell you is that the "incredible odds" are largely *yourself.* Your procrastination, your excuses, your self-doubt, your 1,000 acts of daily sabotage.

Of course, the getting over yourself bit starts earlier than sharing your message or skills on a wider stage. It starts with a more private confidence. With the ability to address the skeptics in your own personal sphere...your family, friends, even former coworkers who exist in a different paradigm than you do. Ever get a bit of a shock when someone you know really well says, "I still don't get how people run a business online and actually make money"? Getting over yourself starts with learning to not worry about the people who don't "get" it. Come up with an elevator pitch that's accessible to them, and leave it at that.

On the outside, this looks like shipping your work, no matter what stage of evolution it (or you) is in.

Shit or get off the pot. Make that first site, have that first launch. Talk about your thing. And most importantly, stop worrying about the judgment of others. I know I sound like a broken record, but the fact that you're doing something brave is better than the 99% who never take any action at all.

There's no way around it — if you want to do work that matters, you have to get over yourself.

And it's such a weird little trick of psychology, right? Because if you believe in something, and know the power of it, why would you shy away from sharing it with the world? Why would you speak exuberantly with your close friends and partners about the things you believe in and care about deeply, but use a soft voice bordering on an apology when bringing it up in front of an audience?

Did Brené Brown whisper about shame?
Did Mark Manson apologize for not giving a fuck?
Did Paul Jarvis mention his veganism under his breath (and only once or twice)?
Did Jenny Lawson, the infamous Bloggess, hide her struggle with mental illness?

No.

How can you ever expect to make a difference, to help another human being, if you don't show us who you are and what you stand for?

You don't need to be some boisterous attention-seeking boob about it. None of the people I listed above are.

Learn from the people who are modeling the sharing of their wisdom well. Randi Buckley, Roxane Gay, Fabeku Fatunmise, Rachel Rodgers, and David Cain all come to mind.

You're not bothering us when you show us who you are and what you stand for.

You're allowing us to choose you.

And yes, it takes emotional energy to put yourself out there.

But the squeaky wheel gets the grease. Time and again, people who may not even be as effective or professional as you or have the same level of integrity that you do are skipping circles around you, business-wise, because they're out there beating their drum louder. Maybe they're more shameless than you, more pushy, more seemingly self-serving than you. But that doesn't mean that you have to do it like that to be successful in this new(ish) online economy!

I tell ya, if I see one more post about a six-figure launch I'm going to scream. All you've told me is that you've made yourself richer. All you've confirmed is that the individualistic obsession with wealth accumulation is still strong in Western society. And look, I have no problem whatsoever with wealth generation and individual success. But how we communicate those stories is so old and boring. What's way more interesting to me is *the change you are effecting*.

Are you just helping more people gain more personal wealth through the latest tactics? It's a fucking snore. I'm admittedly a bit conflicted about writing on this topic because businesses, by their nature, should be profitable. Nobody goes into business to be poor or go into debt. And it's easy for creatives to shy away from owning that they want to make money and that there's nothing shameful about making a healthy profit...even becoming wealthy! But when the sole indicator of success — as all these lifestyle empowerment brands keep shouting from the rooftops — is a six-figure launch or a seven-figure year, we completely lose sight of what we got into business for. When the focus is on numbers generated rather than transformations created, we've got it backwards.

The loudest voices...these squeaky wheels — yes, what you might think of as the most "shameless" marketers — will always get the most attention. So how about we change that? How about we step up and become the new wave of marketers who aren't shamelessly selling and trying to hit income targets. *Your customers aren't income targets!*

Side note: keep in mind that the squeaky wheel doesn't need to be you as the talking head. You get to choose your personal visibility. (What up, introverts!) The squeaky wheel could simply be your message. And if that's the case, as has been the case with many, many successful entrepreneurs, you need to ask yourself, "How is my *message visibility*? And what can I do to improve it?"

Because if your message is galvanizing, transformative, and powerful, it should be given its own drumbeat. It's not only your job, but your privilege, to amplify the reach of something that has the power to change people's perspectives, and by extension, even if in the minutest of ways, their lives.

The Relationship Economy

OK FRIEND, WE'VE NOW PEELED BACK many layers of the Matrix. You can't unsee what you've seen — what we've seen together — as we've peered back into the boxed-in universe we never quite felt a part of.

We've also walked through the valley of risk and uncertainty, giving everything a good, hard science-and-biology-informed side-eye. You've had the chance to rethink things. To start redesigning your relationship with risk. And the exhale feels nice, doesn't it? Freeing, really.

Now we're going to talk about what this new landscape of business actually looks like, and what the stakes are for you, personally, professionally, and globally. It's one thing to wax poetic about a relationship economy because we like things that give us the warm fuzzies.

But WTF does it actually mean?

What does it look like in practice?

What do you have to give up? (Hint: nothing.)

I've got only good news for you, so keep reading.

The Transactional Economy

OK, so we all know how business works, right? It is, at its core, a transactional process.

It's transactional. I have a Thing. You want this Thing. You pay me for the Thing and we both run off with the thing we wanted. Me with your money. You with the Thing you paid me for.

And when the time comes to scale production of the Thing in demand, you choose the cheapest possible production avenue to maximize profit.

Unfortunately, this very paradigm leads to the rich getting richer and the poor getting poorer. We know this...because we've drunk the Kool-Aid. Most of us believe that this is just The Way It Is.

Similar to how we find it hard to envision a future completely devoid of cars running on fossil fuels, we struggle to envision anything other than our current version of capitalism, which leaves disparity and environmental destruction in its wake. Because people are assholes and we want to protect what we think is rightfully ours. Our stuff, our power, me, me, me.

This reeks of bullshit. Well, not the part about people wanting to protect what they believe is rightfully theirs — that rings pretty true to me.

But rather, the bullshit part is this old paradigm of the transactional economy. Just because it's the dominant way we do commerce doesn't mean it's the only version, nor does it mean we have to continue that way in the future.

Women not being allowed to vote used to be the dominant/accepted reality. It's not anymore.

Single-use plastics used to be the dominant/accepted reality. That's changing fast.

Same goes for working for the same company for your whole life, racial inequality, the idea that everybody needs to go to college, gas-powered cars being the primary means of transport, living in the suburbs with 2.5 kids as "the ideal"...even burnout, which was previously accepted as more or less "adulting" and is now recognized by the WHO as a legit syndrome.

Old paradigms that don't feel right are meant to be challenged.

If there's one non-negotiable prerogative of being human, it's that we constantly evolve.

And that's part of the reason we're witnessing the slow sideways slip of the transactional economy. I won't say it's a decline or a demise, because as long as we have greed we'll have some people trying to extract as much as possible from others for minimal cost. But it's certainly a time of reckoning.

So if you're an integrity-driven person with something to share who thinks they'd never want to go into business because they see this model that's dominated by old industrialists, '80s-era Wolves of Wall Street, and click-funnel dude-bros, you're in luck. Because this new wave of capitalism is up to something totally different. And we can exist irrespective of this old paradigm. Hell, we can exist and thrive *in spite of it*.

And that's where the relationship economy comes in.

The relationship economy is a way of engaging in commerce that respects humans over commodities. It values the transformational over the transactional.

This isn't some hippie-dippie bullshit. It's about the impact of where we choose to invest our money, as well as how we choose to show up in return for other people's money.

You know this already.

I can buy a 10-pack of Dove soap for $10.88 at Walmart. Or I can buy three bars for $5 from a soapmaker on Etsy.

I can hire a VA in the Philippines for $10/hour to do grunt work, or I can hire someone closer to home with a more aligned skill set for what I need and pay fair market value.

And don't tell me, "Oh, but Heather, I'm empowering a woman to work for herself in the Philippines!"

I'm calling BS, because that's not likely your motivation. Keeping costs low in your business cannot be masked by the thinness of the "this is a great wage for someone 'over there'" rationalization.[3]

---

3 It's akin to the maddening refrain I used to hear from dudes I knew who went to the skeezy Eastern European strip joint at the edge of town that "most strippers really are empowered by their work and putting themselves through college!" Right, Dave. Whatever.

But I digress.

In the relationship economy, transactions still happen but within the context of a relationship. And that's what makes them transformational.

In the relationship economy, people come first. You're not just selling widgets, you're seeing how your product or service helps someone do, be, or have something different.

You come to your work with a fundamental respect for people's money, time, and humanity.

As a consumer, this means questioning and/or rejecting things like fast fashion. Or unethically produced meat.

As a service or product provider, this looks like having integrity/ following through, paying fair-market wages to people who help you run your business, and showing up on time — every time. And importantly, believing in your product or service to help the end user truly do, be, or have something different...something *better* for themselves.

It means being discerning.

Which is another way of standing in the value of respecting people's time, money, and humanity. It's not the easy way, it's not the most low cost, but it's a shift that we must make individually to contribute to the whisper of change. I dare say it's our job to make that whisper louder.

And, to clarify, this doesn't mean that you flip the transactional economy on its head and you become the one who loses. It doesn't mean you'll be shunned if you don't buy artisan-made soap. It doesn't mean you need to over-deliver or sacrifice your own well-being for the sake of your end user.

It means that you do what's best for both you and the clients. In other words, it's an economic ecosystem in which respect goes both ways, always.

"But Heather, I have to scale my business if I want to survive... and I can't scale in the relationship economy! The math just doesn't work!"

Look, this approach doesn't mean that you necessarily have an individual relationship with every client or buyer. You might not know every one of the 1,000 people in your course or online community (and you're certainly not responsible for each of their feelings), but approaching your audience with that human-to-human approach changes everything. It's the difference between seeing people as cash piñatas versus seeing them as people.

Take, for example, Tara McMullin's online community, What Works. There's no way she knows everyone in there personally. But everyone kind of feels like she might, because she's intentionally put really high-touch community managers in place so that every member feels taken care of. They also have a really well-written set of Community Guidelines which make it feel like a safe and supportive space. I even had a complaint a while ago about another member, and while he hadn't directly offended, he was like a shark in the water. They took me very seriously and though he stayed in the community for a while, he has now vacated the premises and it's entirely possible he was given the boot. The structure of what you build has the power to allow for transformational over transactional.

Building a business guided by the principles of the relationship economy also frees you up from having to be perfect — because now you can be human. It allows you to be flawed, and also asks that you fix that flaw in a way that delights your end user and creates a loyalty to your brand that only comes from you showing up fully and doing the right thing.

A perfect example of this is the online retailer, Zappos. Their tagline is "Powered by Service." And their mission statement, as posted on their About page, is as follows:

> Twenty years ago, we began as a small online retailer that only sold shoes. Today, we still sell shoes — as well as clothing, handbags, accessories, and more. That "more" is providing the very best customer service, customer experience, and company culture. We aim to inspire the world by showing it's possible to simultaneously deliver happiness to customers, employees, the community, and vendors in a long-term, sustainable way.
>
> We hope that in the future people won't even realize we started selling shoes online. Instead, they'll know Zappos as a service company that just happens to sell _____.

A service company.

These guys were practically ground zero for the relationship economy. I recall back when they started, being shocked that an Internet retailer would allow free returns. It was unheard of.

And yet, free returns for things you purchase online is now expected. It would be weird and indeed you'd lose customers *fast* if you made them pay for returns. Because it's not respecting my dollars as a consumer. I'm putting my trust in you as an online retailer that you're representing your products accurately, and that you're providing correct guidance in terms of fit, so that I can choose the right thing. And if when it arrives it's not what I had hoped for, I expect that I'll be able to "return it to the shelf" so to speak.

We never used to have these expectations, but it took companies like Zappos to implement forward-thinking policies that put the consumer first, that respected her dollars, to start that sea change that has become the new norm.

The flip side: maintaining the relationship economy when things go sideways.

After a challenging situation I experienced while working on an expedition ship, a mentor of mine John McKeon said to me, "It doesn't matter what you do when things are going well, what matters is what you do when the shit hits the fan."

On February 23rd, 2014, I was on said ship en route to Antarctica, in a massive storm of near-hurricane force. The waves were averaging 12 meters. As if that weren't cookie-tossing enough, one of the waves was so powerful that it smashed into the side of the vessel and took out three inch-thick plate-glass windows, doing huge damage to the interior and causing water to pour into the main lounge of the ship through the large hole where the windows used to be.

It was a freak accident that made a bad situation even worse, and the roughly 110 guests were on lockdown in their cabins, realizing quickly that their dream vacation was anything but. We managed, after 12 long hours of bobbing slowly through this violent tempest, to turn the vessel safely and get back to the protected waters of the Beagle Channel in Argentina.

What happened over the ensuing hours, days, and months was what proved to me first hand that it doesn't matter how "good" you are when things are going well. What matters is how you show up when the shit hits the fan.

John's company, Polar Latitudes, did everything right. I was on the front lines as the Passenger Service Manager dealing with some angry, exhausted, mildly traumatized guests on the ship. I spent a full 18 hours on my feet serving an seemingly endless line of very disappointed guests while my colleagues handed me sandwiches for sustenance, and I was completely empowered by the company to do whatever possible to help the guests figure out next steps now that their trip had been canceled due to a gaping hole in the side of the ship.

The company was relatively new, and yet that didn't stop them from chartering a plane to fly all guests back to Buenos Aires free of charge, so they could catch international flights back home. They also offered guests the option of coming back the following season on the same trip, in their same cabin, with a $1,000 discount on the price. I could go on, but suffice it to say that treating guests with this level of respect and care is not necessarily an industry standard and this was above and beyond what I'd seen other companies do.

And the best part of this story? We had a 50% return rate from this group of passengers the following season. I was onboard with the returning folks and I asked them what made them decide to sail with us again after such a harrowing experience.

They said that now that they'd seen how we behave in a crisis, they knew they were in excellent hands and wouldn't sail with anyone else. Boom.

"OK, I'm almost convinced. But what about the whole, 'it's just business, it's not personal' thing?"

Here's an unpopular opinion for ya. The "it's just business, it's not personal" thing is *such* bullshit. Maybe it didn't used to be personal, but look where that got us! Ah gawd...this is like old white capitalist speak and I ain't buying it! I truly believe that if you think that way, you're a dinosaur, and you're going to be left in the dust.

The minute you say, "It's not personal, it's just business," you remove the human from the equation. It's another way of saying, "Sorrynotsorry you just got jacked over. It's not personal." Gross!

Business *is* personal. At least in my ecosystem it is, and will always be. I'm stating this as truth because I decided it's my truth and you can do the same. This is how we *be the change*, friend.

Look, people have different expectations now. The market has evolved. As consumers, we've been given a taste of respect and humanity, and we're not interested in going backward.

When I talk about the 9-to-5, I talk a lot about having broken out of the Matrix. How you can't unsee what you've now seen. And as consumers, we've *also* started breaking out of the Matrix. You can't unsee the freedom of choice and respect for your dollars. Like the example I shared before about how we used to have to pay return fees for online purchases and now that's a ridiculous concept.

So, to recap...

The transactional economy is soulless. It is purely trade-based and does not take into account any living beings involved. Because of this lack of soul, the result of a transactional economy is that the 1% continues to accumulate the most, while the 99% sinks lower in both material and mental health and well-being.

The relationship economy is still transaction-based, but it requires us to see each other. It brings our humanness into the deal. Rather than being an empty transaction, it's a transfer of goods or services that fully respects the entities on each end of the exchange. Even if there may be imbalances in some transactions, no one is getting screwed in the relationship economy.

In general terms: the transactional economy is exploitative and extractive. The relational economy is generative and restorative.

So here we're going to start transitioning into the bigger stakes. I know you're probably thinking, "Well, this feels nice to consider, but it's some pretty John-and-Yoko shit you're talking about here."

But here's the deal: change always begins with smaller groups and communities starting to adopt different practices. I'm not asking you to reinvent the wheel here, or do the impossible. I'm asking you to be one of the people on the leading edge of a necessary revolution.

Because we can't continue on doing things the way we've been doing them. The system is so beyond broken, as we can clearly see from the growing chasm between the super rich and the masses of increasingly poor. We can't continue on accepting things as "good enough."

We should be modeling relationship economy behaviour for our kids so that they grow up with those values and can carry the torch, even if they work in the traditional working world. Our little people can observe us *seeing each other* and know that that's the world they want to live in. Just like I grew up in Canada with our hard-core politeness and as a result I'm polite to the point where it's almost annoying, even when it's not reciprocated, because that's how I grew up and *that's the world I want to live in.*

Put simply: if you work with humans, I believe this is the way forward.

We desperately need a kinder ecosystem for commerce. And given that the transactional economy makes the rich richer and pisses everyone else off, it's high time we evolve into a way of doing business that works better for all of us.

And how do we do that, specifically? I'm so glad you asked...

Creating a business culture in the relationship economy

Whether you're a company of one, or a few, or many, creating a culture where the business is personal comes from the top. This is one truism that cannot be circumvented. We've probably all worked in places where we wanted to do good things — the right things — yet management wasn't interested in anything much beyond fulfilling the transactional. And if the boss ain't into it, it ain't going to happen.

About the only thing I liked about my pharmaceutical job is that I had a lot of autonomy. One of the medicines I promoted was for overactive bladder (a condition largely suffered by the elderly) and the topic of cognitive impairment was always a part of the conversation.

Many patients suffered from some form of dementia and this medication could make their confusion worse. Given that my district encompassed the largely Spanish-speaking area of Toronto, I soon discovered that there were a lot of families who were managing an elderly parent with cognitive disabilities and trying to navigate an English-based medical system with Spanish as their native language.

I asked if I could use some funding to pull together a Spanish-language information day for families at one of the elderly care facilities, and I contacted the Alzheimer's Society in the US to send me a couple of boxes of information in Spanish. (Keep in mind I'm from Canada, and any "alternate language" brochures produced by large orgs like the Alzheimer's Society are usually in French.) I brought in a well-respected Spanish-speaking geriatrician to talk to the families and it was a really nice day.

I can't say that this event directly led to any increase in my sales, but it certainly helped my relationship with the Spanish-speaking medical community that I promoted the event to, because I wasn't trying to sell them shit. I was actually trying to help them close a knowledge gap with their community as well as help the families better understand their loved one's condition.

This is the kind of stuff that allowed me to sleep at night, in a job that I otherwise felt was soul-sucking, and my superiors were really impressed with my initiative. But that's where the buck stopped. I got kudos (big deal) and then everyone went back to trying to drive up sales numbers.

Now, I'm not so naive as to expect that a pharma company, of all kinds, would ever treat the business as personal. They're some of the worst culprits in the transactional business universe.

But my point is that when *you* are the type of person who sees the business as personal, you'll always feel stunted when you're working within an organization where the people at the top take a transactional approach.

Because the people at the top are the culture-makers. And if you're a company of one, *you're* the culture-maker.

The way you make people *feel* when they interact with your business, the way you empower others with your services or products, the way they experience your brand as an individual...those are the effects of the culture you create.

There's a small company I know of in the polar tourism industry that was once known as churning out the best of the best, the most professional, the most qualified guides — but then they started losing their best talent. Bit by bit, the attrition started to show. Why? Because other companies were raising rates and paying them much better... *paying them what they were worth.*

Because the people in this small company's head office didn't treat the business as personal.

They didn't recognize that their end product, the very thing they were selling, was the experience that was delivered by their crack team of highly skilled guides. They knew other companies were paying more but they refused to budge, still calling themselves "the best company to work for" and expecting their guides to work just as hard for much less pay than they could command elsewhere.

Here's a tip: Loyalty comes in part when you treat people fairly. And if the values at the top aren't in line with that, you'll feel it all the way through the organization.

It's the exact same in any small business. It's on you to make sure that your touchpoints with your collaborators, contractors, and end users are designed around your values.

You set the tone.

Remember when we were young and naive, believing that social change could happen in our lifetime if we could just get enough of a groundswell to influence politicians to make better planet- and human-focused decisions?

Haha! Haaaaaaa. Hahaha. Hah.

And then we grew up.
And felt the pain of disillusionment.
And searched for answers, for pathways.
And got discouraged.
And then saw a little bit of progress. (Like major cities banning plastic bags.)
And then witnessed a whole lot of regression. (Ahem, Trump.)

But in the midst of all this, something happened that decentralized the voices of power. We got the Internet.

The past two decades have given us not only this phenomenal tool but also a massive, evolving connective landscape to play with and share ideas in. And most importantly, it put *agency* back in our hands.

It gives us the space to develop our own economies. To develop commercial ecosystems that don't exploit. To co-create the relationship economy we know we need to shift the tide and look for solutions to all the stuff that's been broken by centralized wealth and power.

I know this sounds really pie-in-the-sky, but we are a much larger and more massive force than we realize. There are literally hundreds of thousands of people out there, if not many more, that find the inequalities we are currently forced to accept intolerable.

Things like only getting two weeks of vacation a year.
And the appallingly short (anti-human-well-being) maternity leave "granted" in most countries.
And the bullshit policies and attitudes that people of colour encounter every. single. day.
And pay gaps.
And destruction of irreplaceable environments for profit.

And access to healthcare.
And debt. (Fucking debt!)

Basically, everything that's keeping us from a healthy world.

Truth be told, there's a sickness here that has allowed things to get this way in the first place. A sickness based not only in the big bad bears of greed and individualism but in this simmering natural push we have inside all of us, which is to protect ourselves before we extend that protection to anyone else. I'm certainly guilty of it. And let's be honest, we can't expect to change anything until we're willing to look the problem straight in the eyeballs.

Just like you, I want to live comfortably and maintain, if not increase, the standard of living I grew up with.
Just like you, I don't want to give up my creature comforts and conveniences.
Just like you, I want to feel safe at all times.
And just like you, I don't want to retain those things *at the expense of others or the environment.*

But in most scenarios, we aren't given much of a choice because the current economic structure is fucked. And it's precisely because of our connectivity that we're starting to wake up to this on a different level.

Now we're feeling that the pain of staying the same has become greater than the pain of change. And change we will.

By choosing to do things differently, you are opting out of this broken structure and — make no mistake — changing the system. This is an insanely exciting time to live in!

In theory, the relationship economy doesn't leave space for anyone to be left behind. It doesn't have room for the massive gaps and inequalities we currently have. It doesn't see race, gender, or geographical barriers.

And if everyone is respected and valued, *culture shifts*.

You can help fix what's busted. You can contribute meaningfully. Yes, you and your little business. Because changes in the micro *are* changes in the macro.

You doing what you do shows other people what's possible.

Pretty damn cool that you get to do it by running a business, eh?

Because remember, that's what this whole thing is ultimately about. Our ass-kicking, world-changing selves aren't just out there saving the world, we're also making enough money to support ourselves and, ideally, get our best work out in the world.

As I've said before, entrepreneurship is just the medium.

Which means that if you do want to get that magical combo of world-saving, money-making, genius-tapping business going, you have to figure out what your business is really about.

When we think about business as a medium for social change, most of us assume we have to be running a non-profit, or an entity that specifically tackles a social issue, like sex trafficking or body negativity.

But that's not what I'm talking about here. I'm talking about businesses that foster social change by operating with a different *ethos*. Businesses that give a big middle finger to the for-profit-only model.

Take Bob's Red Mill. I heard founder Bob Moore speak at the 2013 World Domination Summit and I haven't been able to shake the power of his story since. If you're not familiar with Bob's Red Mill, it's a whole-grain food producer with a really cool business model. Bob had many employees who had worked for him upwards of 30 years so, on his 81st birthday, he surprised his employees by announcing an Employee Stock Ownership Program (ESOP), which essentially made everyone right down to the janitor an employee-owner. Meaning, when the company does well, every single employee benefits.

Or we can look at a different business model in our polar expedition company. Sure, we're a tourism operator, but the way we approach our business is that we deliver a transformational experience. People come on holiday and leave better educated about our changing polar regions but also passionate about their incomparable beauty and fragility. We bake our values into the experience our guests have with us.

Here's the thing: your business is just the medium for delivering your genius/the change you want to see/the values you want to share, etc. to the world.

Bob's Red Mill isn't about grains. It's a family/values-based business that happens to sell grains.

Our polar expedition company isn't about tourism. It's an experience-delivery business that happens to provide small-vessel expeditions to the Norwegian Arctic.

My consulting business isn't about revenue growth and sales targets. It's a holistic professional (and personal!) development experience that happens to offer strategic growth support for entrepreneurs.

Your turn.

What type of business do you run (or want to run), and *what do you truly deliver?*

Seriously, grab a piece of paper and fill in these blanks:

I run a _____ business that happens to offer

_____.

If your eyes are spinning around in opposite directions...

Don't worry. If you read all of this and thought, "Heather, WTF, these are massive questions," you're right! It's OK if you don't know exactly what your thing is yet. This is all part of what it means to become an entrepreneur (instead of just learning a business model).

And that's what this book is all about. We're just about to get into how you actually learn who you are as an entrepreneur — and it's good stuff. But for now, maybe take a little break. Drink some water. And get ready...because we're about to dive even deeper.

PART 2

WHO YOU NEED TO BE

Owning Your Shit

YOU KNOW HOW SOME (MOST) DAYS you feel like you can accomplish almost anything, and then other days you're like, "What in the hell am I thinking?!?"

I hear you.

I *am* you.

And this chapter is all about helping you get a grip on the what-the-hell-am-I-thinking aspect of entrepreneurship.

If you've made it this far without chucking this book in the trash, then the ideas I've shared here, like the relationship economy and creating ecosystems so that business is better for everyone, are clearly resonating with you.

This isn't anything new. I didn't invent these concepts. But it is a call to action for all of you with even the smallest modicum of agency to step up and start to be the change.

You're well on your way to learning who you are as an entrepreneur, and (in true entrepreneur fashion) this probably means that you've got a lot of big ideas about the possibilities for your work and its impact in the world.

And THAT. IS. GREAT.

I am so fucking excited for you.

Now is your time.

If you'd become an entrepreneur in the '80s with almost no capital, the chances of you making an impact would have been minuscule in comparison to what's available to you now at no or low cost.

Inasmuch as you have a limitless sandbox to play in as an entrepreneur in these times, I have no doubt your subconscious gremlin has been hanging around uninvited and taken a few craps in your proverbial sandbox.

Yup. Big turds. In your sandbox. The kind that don't go away by themselves. You've gotta do the dirty work of rooting them out, picking them up (eww), and giving them the ol' heave-ho. Or at least putting them in a little pile over in the corner so you can keep an eye on them.

So before you get too bananas over your big dreams and the possibilities of making that pie-in-the-sky stuff happen, you have to start out by doing something much less sexy: owning your shit.

Why you have to own your shit *first*

"Ughhh booo Heather, why? Why can't I just dream big and plan a business and just fucking do it? Why do I have to do all this introspection stuff? I'm not into this self-help kumbaya business. I just want to get 'er done using the shortest line from A to B!"

I know, I know. I'm the same! I'm an action-taker. I don't have time for spiritual journeys.

But as I've said before: the biggest barrier to making whatever you want to happen is you. So you can either deal with your shit proactively, with your eyes wide open, or you can ignore your shit and it'll all come back to bite you anyway.

Bottom line: you cannot escape your own damn self.

You can't escape the psychological turds in your sandbox. Wouldn't you rather know they've been identified and piled in the corner, rather than dig up an unpleasant surprise when you're building your castles?

We all know that our subconscious's favourite pastime is making up a lot of shit to (supposedly) keep ourselves safe. And that means you've got a lot of introspection work to do to become more keenly aware of your strengths and weaknesses. Otherwise you'll likely end up spinning your wheels, running out of money, buying a bunch of courses or hiring specialists you don't need thinking they'll be the golden ticket, and on and on and on. I hate to generalize, but I've seen this with my own eyes for so many years that it warrants a whole chapter of a book to address it!

You can't build a thriving business (which includes building yourself as an entrepreneur) by doing a bunch of courses and following everybody else's methods when you still have all your un-dealt-with shit on the inside, sabotaging you.

How can I be so certain about this? Because you've never *been* an entrepreneur before (or not yet achieved wild success as one). You've been a human, sure. But that requires you to interact with people in a fairly smallish set of ways. You've not yet armed yourself with the mindset and skill set it takes to show up every day in this new adaptation as an entrepreneurial human. These are two very different planes of existence.

As a regular human, there's no requirement to hold a bigger-picture vision in your personal life. It's nice, but not necessary. Yet there's an *absolute necessity* for it in business. And you can't do that if you don't own your shit first.

It's kind of like being a parent. Before you become a parent, you've never been a parent before. You can't possibly know what it's like...nor how this new identity forces you to grow, change, compromise, and expand in ways you didn't see coming.

But we can start by recognizing our shortcomings and working to improve them. Whether as a new parent for the sake of our children ("What's at the root of my impatience?") or as a new entrepreneur for the sake of our business ("What's at the root of my lack of follow-through?").

You'll be tempted to just gloss over this...but let me tell you, you've got stakes in the game and ignoring this is one of the quickest routes back into the trappings of what you've long wanted to escape from. As I've said before, people who don't do the internal work are generally the ones that don't make it.

Yes, it's scary, uncomfortable, and frustrating, but if you avoid it, then not only do you not get to live as fully as you truly want for yourself, your work doesn't get out to the world, and other people don't get to benefit from it.

Case in point: earlier today I was supporting a client who was going through the awkward transition of breaking ties with a contractor who hadn't been pulling his weight. It was awkward because they'd become friends over the course of working together and my client was worried about deeply upsetting him. (There had been indications that he wouldn't take it well.)

It all worked out relatively fine in the end, but my client said she used to keep difficult discussions more ambiguous or open-ended so as not to upset others (sandbox turd right there) and now she didn't take others' reactions to heart as much as she would have a couple of years back. "That sort of thing used to completely undo me," she stated in a text message. But these days? She's levelled up. She can handle herself as a boss and uphold boundaries in a kind and firm manner that's in line with the entrepreneur that she is. She's done the hard work. Heck, she's *doing* the hard work of becoming.

And that's exactly the kind of owning your shit I'm talking about. Let's dig a little deeper...

OK, so what does owning your shit actually look like?

Now that I've got you primed to go into your inner sandbox, I'm going to be talking about two types of owning your shit in this chapter: the internal messiness and the external expressions.

The internal shit you need to own is the stuff that fuels your resistance to doing work that matters. It's your sense of (or lack of) worthiness, competence, confidence, and ownership, among many other things.

You've absolutely got to stare these beasts in the face because if not, they'll pull you under on a moment's notice — and hold you down, make no mistake.

The external shit you need to own is all related to the authentic expression of yourself in the public sphere. I know, that word "authentic" needs a fork stuck in it — but it's important. You need to own your quirks, your nerdiness, your unpopular opinions, and the bigger-picture stuff that galvanizes you. And unless you deal with the internal first, you're not going to have the personal capacity to own your space in the public sphere.

Let's unpack each of these a little more.

The internal shit

When you start down this road of living a life more closely aligned with your values, all kinds of crap comes up.

Generally speaking I've seen two versions of "new entrepreneur syndrome" play out.

VARIATION ONE

People who really struggle with worthiness, or taking their proverbial seat at the table. This is rooted in what I call comparisonitis. The inner dialogue around this looks like different variations of the following:

I don't have anything good to say.
Why would anyone listen to me?
Why would anyone read my work/take my course/buy my product?

Who am I fooling?

Why would anyone hire me as their therapist/photographer/agent?

There are so many people ahead of me in the game, I can't possibly "hang my shingle out" until I'm as accomplished and polished as they are.

If people do hire me, what if I fail? What if I can't deliver what they expect?

OMG Emily Entrepreneur's site looks so much better than mine...she must be better at what she does...

This is a frustrating loop to be in because you're your own barrier to getting your work out there. Your thoughts are completely undermining your ability to build something that matters. In fact, it's more than undermining. It's paralyzing.

VARIATION TWO

People who feel pretty good about what they have to offer in the beginning. They're more confident than average out of the gate, put together a business concept and website, and then get a total kick in the pants when they hear crickets at launch time.

This is an equally frustrating loop because you've taken the steps, you've reviewed the data again and again, and can't see what's wrong. So you start beating yourself up thinking you're not good enough, you can't compete, you're an idiot because you didn't figure out how to reach your target audience before you spent all the time and money building the thing you want to sell.

I'm generalizing a lot here but you get the picture. The common denominator here is you *blaming yourself*. For not being good enough, not being savvy enough, not having enough money to invest, not knowing what you don't know, not looking polished enough and, and, and...

And you know what blame is? Utterly fucking useless. It's not going to get you anywhere except set further back.

We also have a lot of freak-out thoughts about what's possible. What if your business, ideas, or movement does go big? What if you write a book or build a community and then *have to be accountable*? What if you get haters? Faaack!

Which brings me to *visibility*.

Not everyone wants to be in the public sphere. And even if you guard your privacy with the force of a thousand Jedis, your name will still be associated with your work. A lot of people feel freaked out by being more visible, possibly making mistakes, feeling unprepared to show up in any way that's less than perfect, etc. etc. etc. (I can hear your monkey mind taking this and running with it...)

And hey, while we're at it, let's keep naming shit! *Capacity*. We both underestimate and fear our own capacity, leaving us stuck in this ugly tension of "There's no way I can do this" and "Oh shit, what if I do accomplish this and then I have to actually follow through?" A lot of being a baby entrepreneur is ping-ponging back and forth between these two states every few minutes or so, which is tiring and often paralyzing.

Of course, we can't forget my very favourite: judgment. Mother of pearl, are we crippled by the (perceived) judgment of others or what? In fact, you can forget about anything else I listed before this, because if you're worried about what others will think, that's your biggest problem by a long shot and needs to be your focus for the foreseeable future.

I hate to sound like a broken record, but this isn't a *you* issue. Yes, you need to do the work to reverse it, but you are not the root of these issues. This is a society and schooling issue.

Because we're taught by society and by school that there's a direct correlation between effort and reward. You work hard on deliverables, you get XYZ. You follow the system, and things work out. There is no requirement for you to do emotional labour, according to what you've been taught. There's no expectation of personal investment or growth. Cogs in the wheel are just cogs. Easy peasy. Serve a function.

But that doesn't exist in entrepreneurship.

There is no direct line from effort to profit. *And everything about who you are gets called into question in the space between the two.*

Think about it: when you're six months into blogging and still nobody gives a shit, how do you keep going? Or when your launch flops? Or when your product gets delayed at the factory and your wholesale customers get pissed?

As a business owner, you must be able to keep going — ideally with grace and calm — in the face of unexpected outcomes. And you can only do that if you have your internal stuff sorted.

One last thing that's critical about living a life and building a business based on your values is that it requires you to stand behind them unflinchingly. And yet it can be super hard to stand up for our values, even the ones we hold dear, because societal pressure, humans, weirdness, whatever. Part of your internal work is learning to stand in that power.

Just think of how few people stand up to their (drunk) racist uncle at

Thanksgiving, even if internally they're screaming about the injustice of his rants.

"Don't want to rock the boat."
"This isn't the time or place."
"My opinion won't change anything."

As an entrepreneur, your work is rocking boats. Your time is now. Your opinion, your decisions about how to steer your ship, has the power to change many things, simply by serving as a lighthouse for those that come after you, if nothing else.

OK, so what do I do?

I know business books are supposed to be super motivating; I'm supposed to assure you that by reading this book, I'll share a shortcut to getting what you want (if you just learn My Proprietary Secret™). But I'm afraid I have to disappoint.

The reality is, there's no easy way through this. There's no 5-Step System. You can't schedule your breakthroughs. You can't become this levelled-up version of yourself where you don't suffer the slings and arrows of your own negative thought spirals without doing the work.

I mean, it's freaking hard to face up to this internal stuff on a normal human regular-life basis, much less when you're in the flurry of amygdala activation that is entrepreneurship.

The good news is that fear and action can coexist. (I learned that the oh-shit way by jumping out of an airplane back in 2005. But that's a story for another time.)

Thing is, we seem to have bought this line that you have to be fearless to do great work. That "successful people" have harnessed some kind of unstoppable confidence. That's simply not the case. Rather, what they've done is acknowledged their weaknesses and *acted from their strengths.*

This is the brilliant secret of normal humans doing extraordinary things: you can get really honest about your foibles and weaknesses, and still make the choice to act in accordance with your values, because owning the cracks in your armor makes you stronger. In becoming an entrepreneur, you are being called to both acknowledge your weaknesses and act from your strengths. It's a genius combo of acceptance and action that'll make you unstoppable, not some nonexistent superhumanness.

And since you have this human brain, with all of its hangups, now is the time to shift into acceptance/action mode. Every day, when those undermining thoughts come up, you say, "No. No no no no no. We're not playing this bullshit game."

It's not what people want to hear. Behaviour change is unsexy, it's annoying, and it takes a really long time. But that is your job, if you wanna do stuff that matters. I'm a huge fan of the car metaphor. You're in the driver's seat, your fear/anxiety/whatever is in the passenger seat, and you're fully aware that She. Is. Right. There.

Right there next to you. Being a pain in the ass. Talking crap directly into your ear. And your job is to say, "I see you. I know you're there. I can hear you, feel you, smell you. But I am the one driving. I'm not entertaining your BS right now."

You'll have to say this again and again and again. Sometimes multiple times a day on particularly challenging days. Practice it. Create the habit.

Own that you are in the driver's seat.

Because once you know that your fear/anxiety/monkey mind/lack of confidence is always lingering nearby, you can work on your relationship with it (because let's be honest, it's not likely ever going to go away). And yet, it doesn't have to ever take the wheel from you. Really take that in: your fear can never *take* the wheel from you. You can (and will) give it to her. But that's the only way she can get it. And you can always take it back. This is your one most important job as an entrepreneur: keeping control of the wheel. And it's something you have to learn by doing.

The advantage of disadvantages

So, we've covered some areas that require you to roll up your sleeves and make some effort. But now I want to dial it back for a minute and talk about a part of becoming that'll be easy for you: how the things that make it hard for people like us to fit into the Matrix are huge advantages in entrepreneur-land.

Things like:

- Having a short attention span
- Having lots of ideas
- Having the ability to focus like crazy on one thing that you're interested in for a delineated period of time
- Being a fast mover/get shit done-er
- Having a strong desire for work autonomy
- Being allergic to inefficient people or processes
- Being impatient with people who don't take personal responsibility

All of these are the worst when you're trying to fit into the 9-to-5.

I know you feel me. But these disadvantages in the workplace are the things that will make you a supernova when you're building your own thing.

Truth be told, that list near perfectly describes me and I had a horrible time trying to fit in to the 9-to-5 as a result. I was often frustrated with my work parameters, my coworkers, and the endless reports we had to put together just to prove to someone up above that we were doing what we were paid to do. Ugh. No thank you. #neveragain

The other aspect that comes into play is how going through shit/trauma/neglect/general bad stuff, especially as a child, really sets you up for success here.

I know it sounds weird. But bear with me.

If you've gone through some shit — i.e., traversed some valleys of despair and managed to come out the other side — you already have a built-in capacity for dealing with things that others aren't prepared for.

Because if this is you, you're likely more resilient than most.
You're more resourceful than most.
You know you can depend on yourself.
You've been to some dark-ass places and your crazy-bar has been raised.

I'd bet my bottom dollar that nothing in entrepreneurship will ever be as dicey as some of the other things you've been through.

I speak from experience. By the age of 17 I had known depths of grief, neglect, isolation, and loneliness that no kid should ever have to encounter. I'd lived in a foreign country where I didn't speak the language, alone with an abusive parent who was only physically present about 50% of the time. I'd been cut off from almost all of my extended family that loved and cared for me as a child. And this was pre-Internet, so the isolation was real. We're talking snail-mail era. While it's true that I had friends and school, the weight on my shoulders of the weirdness of my existence was crushing.

Like most people's stories, it was complicated. And sad. And really maddening for the people who hear the full tale. I developed a lot of coping mechanisms to get through those times. Coping mechanisms that (thank Buddha) turned into strengths as I found my footing as an adult.

If you've been through your own traumas and hard times growing up, you know exactly what I'm talking about. Nothing will be as bad as it was when you were powerless. When you had little to no say over the circumstances of your life. I used to always tell myself that when I grew up, when I was one day free, I would never allow things to be this bad. I'd make great decisions, I'd protect myself, and I'd choose wonderful people to surround myself with. You know that quote, "The creative adult is the child who survived"? Yeah, that.

But hey, if you don't have traumas and shit, that's fine too. A close friend of mine often says you shouldn't have had to suffer to have great skills later in life. And she's right. Simply by virtue of being here, reading this book, there's something different about you. Something that means you can't fit into the Matrix. And being too fast/too weird/too whatever to fit in makes the decision to lean into your entrepreneurial future far easier because you don't have the luxury of a "safe haven" to go back to. You must deal with your shit, or, basically, die (I mean, not really...but this is called the Death Ground Strategy).

I like to think of the process of entrepreneurship along a spectrum, with one end being the "Anxious Annie/Alan" version of you that's new and has soooo much to figure out. On the other end, we have the "Ride or Die, Motherfucker!" version of you. No matter where you begin on the spectrum, the process of becoming who you need to be is consistently moving you closer to the ride-or-die end. It's the ride-or-die end that you long for. And any disadvantages you've had in life will only steel you more for this new iteration of yourself.

So what's your inventory?

Right then, ready to dig in a bit and get an inventory of where you're at internally? Great. This will be your new baseline, your jumping-off point.

Grab a piece of paper or notepad and start by making two lists. Don't skip this bit, no matter where you are on the above-mentioned spectrum, because we're never not growing and there's always some new insight to be gained with this inventory exercise.

So, break out the pen and paper. Old school. Analog. Right-brain activation.

Step 1: Write down your known strengths and weaknesses. Don't overthink it. You already know this shit.

Once you've done this, take a look at those strengths. How can you leverage them in your business? Are there any you've been ignoring or playing down because they don't seem to fit? Chances are there's a way you can use them — and they might just become some of your greatest advantages in business.

And, funny enough, the same thing goes for your weaknesses. Instead of viewing them as inherent character flaws, try to see them as *potential strengths*. You can always get better at something. Or, if you don't want to allocate the time and energy to do that, then you can delegate it as soon as possible and get it off your plate. Either way, you're now able to make a conscious choice of what you do with it.

Step 2: Now let's dive even deeper behind the curtain and get a sense for some character traits you might not know you have. The way I love to do this is to think about your pet peeves. Think about all the people you interact with in your business sphere. What drives you crazy? What do you see people in your field do that really irks you?

Got it? Nice and irritated now? OK, take that feeling and use it as a guide to see how you need to set up your business so you can make sure you focus on the things you really care about. Hate shitty customer service? Use that as inspiration to make sure your value of caring for humans always comes through. Can't stand it when people flake on you? That shows you that you really care about respect in business. You can then build your business to make sure that you incorporate that value into everything you do. For example, you can teach your people how to act respectfully towards you by telling them that you expect them to be on any calls you have together five minutes ahead of time, or adding in a penalty for last-minute cancellations in your contracts. It can be really little things, but by creating the expectation of respect you actually get the results you want.

Long story short: your strengths, weaknesses, and values are your compass. They'll help you know what to focus on, what to work on or delegate, and how to ensure you create a business that's aligned with what you truly care about.

But you can only get to them if you do the internal work.

Take a stand.

Show up.
Show us what you've got.
Be here now, because "the best time to plant a tree" and all that jazz.
You feel me?

The external shit

All right, we've done a *lot* of work so far in this chapter. And we've only covered the internal stuff. But that's OK, because it's the hardest, foundational stuff. If you've got that in the works, the external stuff can't help but evolve as a by-product.

So, let's start by really defining what the external stuff is. **In essence, it's the public expression of your values as shown by your actions.**

Owning your shit externally does not mean that you need to publicize every hot-mess day that you have. What it *does* mean is that you need to show us a true expression of you. We crave authentic — for lack of a less annoying word — expressions of people, and yet we're terrified to tell the truth about ourselves, to be the truest versions of ourselves.

Here we are bitching about being forced to swim in a sea of manufactured personalities, about being surrounded by the bullshit aesthetic of authenticity (I used to be dirt poor and now I'm #livinthedream), and, quite honestly, we're desperate for people to show up strong as themselves.

But what about us? What about the things we don't say? What about the smoke and mirrors we ourselves use in order to fit the narrative?

Nuh uh, friend. Time to own your shit.

Mythology matters

Your mythology, or story, is a critical part of how people know to trust you. You don't have to have a rags-to-riches story or have been a lawyer who became a screenwriter, but you do have to tell us your story. Something. Anything. It shouldn't be lame, but it shouldn't be bullshit either. Don't call yourself self-made unless you're actually self-made. No one appreciates truthiness when they realize what's actually going on there.

Because remember: the business is personal. People hire you for you. People trust your brand because of the values you built it with. People want to hear your, or your business's, story in order to find their connection points. If your story sounds like everyone else's, you're robbing Your People of the opportunity to see that you are The One they should work with/hire/give tons of venture capital to.

Your mythology, your *true story* is another reason you have to do the internal work first. You can't show up as an authentic expression of your values if you don't know what they are or have other psychological shit running rampant and, ultimately, calling the shots for you.

I get that it's hard for us to say things that might be unpopular, to show our true selves, and invite judgment in general in normal life. And then...and then! You tie that true self to your livelihood, going center stage in front of the entire Internet, and you're in total amygdala-land. (gasp - horror - faint #imdead)

But let me lay it out for you in a way that'll feel a lot less freaky.

When I think of owning your shit, I think of two buckets. One bucket is stuff that you feel strongly about that's not part of popular opinion (e.g., I believe the 9-to-5 world is soul-sucking and inhumane) and the other bucket is your inner nerd (e.g., I love the Golden Girls). Things from both of these buckets, when shared out loud, create points of resonance for your audience.

Rather than worrying about what other people think (which is a really unhelpful thing to worry about), worry that the people who are like you *need* you. It's your job to send out the signal flare and be like, "Hey weirdos! Come join my weirdo camp over here so we can be weird together!"

I know most people get nervous when I talk about owning your beliefs that are not part of popular opinion, but it's only scary when you feel like you're the only one. Once you start owning it publicly, you quickly see that you're not the only one because the other people who were nervous about feeling that way come out of the woodwork.

Look, I could be worried about offending people I love a lot with publicly declaring that I believe the 9-to-5 world is soul-sucking and inhumane. I could steer clear of calling myself an atheist for fear of turning spiritual people away. I could be swayed by the stigma of admitting I don't really have a maternal instinct. But the truth is that being honest about that stuff is part of my superpower. People know that they don't have to worry about saying the "wrong" thing about jobs, god, or motherhood around me.

Look at Paul Jarvis, who likes to talk about veganism and his counter-digital-culture belief that you don't have to scale in the traditional sense to be super successful (read his book *Company of One* after this). People who love their red meat and simultaneously want to scale the shit outta their business by creating a Proprietary System™ and then training other people to deliver it are *not* Paul's People.

You feel me?

Even better, I can think of a gazillion examples where owning one's shit directly led to wild success because being public about it helped their tribe find them. But I'll just share a couple of my favourites.

One is the podcast *My Favorite Murder (MFM)*. It's a comedy podcast about murder and it's hilarious. Their followership is *massive*. Followers refer to themselves as Murderinos and they've even broken off into subgroups. My favourite subgroup is called the Schitterinos (people who love *MFM* and the TV show *Schitt's Creek*), which is, at the time of this writing, 11,572 strong. (A subgroup of a niche group, people!)

What I think is so powerful about this is that murder isn't funny, but true crime is fascinating for many people and it can be really depressing to follow true crime stories. So the hosts of *MFM* decided to tell really sad stories but make them lighter by inserting comedic commentary. By their own reports, the throngs of followers of *MFM* are grateful to have found a community where they don't feel ashamed about their interest in true crime and can have a laugh while they learn about the real story behind that serial killer that was prowling around their region in the early '90s.

Even better, the hosts Karen Kilgariff and Georgia Hardstark let it all hang out about the fact that they have had eating disorders, suffer from anxiety, can't pronounce words properly, never went to college, and all kinds of things that we're supposed to feel ashamed of. (Thanks stigma, you arsehole!) They make it OK for their listeners to be imperfect humans with curious interests. How powerful is that?

Karen and Georgia had no idea the podcast concept would be so popular, but now it's turned into a small empire and they even have their own podcast network.

Another example of owning your shit is Denise Duffield-Thomas. She wrote *Get Rich, Lucky Bitch* and turned her teaching around money (and money shame) into an empire. She's super accessible in spite of the fact that she's now a millionaire. In fact, I've known Denise as an online friend since before she wrote the book when she had a rather crappy website. I interviewed her on video for a group coaching program I did in 2012, and we've always been in each other's orbits.

I can honestly say that Denise is just as down to earth now as a millionaire as she was then. She still posts loads of photos of herself without makeup and even wrote a very popular article about the fact that the way she keeps her shit together is by hiring help to do, well, pretty much everything domestic, so that she doesn't have to.

Denise has always been so freaking normal and stood strong when people have criticized her for things like swearing. (Apparently, some folks think that's unprofessional.) She's also not shied away from stating where she stands on political issues. And I respect her a lot for it. She and I share the attitude that "if I'm not for you, no worries. There's the door."

You know what I own? Foraging (it's for hippies) and knitting (it's for old ladies). I mean, how does that jive with being a jet-setting ripped-jeans-and-high-boots-wearing location-independent dual business owner? But I love both with a fiery passion. I collect enough food in the forest every fall to get us through a zombie apocalypse. (And could probably knit everyone new clothes, but it would take a while.)

I'm also a music nerd who studied the North Indian classical drums — the tabla — for six years and who gets absolutely high on analyzing rhythmic cycles in all kinds of genres just as much as I love early Metallica. Most people will read that and be like, "WTF? She's lost me there." But a few of you will be all "HELL YES."

You've gotta own your shit. Seriously. Want a cult of raving fans? Own your shit. Do not apologize for being you, and please for the love of all the gods don't hide yourself. **Don't sanitize your words, your personality, or your message to reach more people or because you're worried about alienating some people that you could help.**

Friend, fuuuuuck that.

Just because you *could* help someone, doesn't mean you're the right person to do it.

Don't martyr your own unique flavour for the sake of the masses. The masses do not give a shit about you. The masses will not be your loyal People. Your loyal People will be your loyal People and they will love the shit out of you for being the real deal. Find the people that think you're so rad they want to tattoo clever things you say on their inner wrist. I'm not even kidding.

Just to remind you...

This is big, hard work. We're currently in the process of following this massive arc of knowing what your big why is and determining the impact of your business. To figure that out, you have to know who you *are*. And how do you do that? You look at your internal stuff, and then how that can be expressed through two external buckets.

Yeah...it's a lot. And, you absolutely can do it.

The best thing is, any action you take is ultimately going to move you further along the Anxious Annie/ride-or-die motherfucker spectrum as long as you continue to view it with that spirit of experimentation we talked about in Chapter 2. It's all just information.

And, as long as you keep doing this and taking actions that are ever-more-aligned with your values, you'll get closer and closer to that big why, too. You'll inevitably move from more vague stuff like "I want to help people" to "I create meaningful connections," etc.

When you do the work, push your strengths (and potential strengths) along the spectrum, you get clarity around what you're about and how you want to show up...which is exactly what we're deep-diving into in the next chapter. :)

Figuring Out *Your* Reasons for Doing This Work

OK, STILL WITH ME? BUELLER?

I know it's all a lot to chew on, but let's recap. We know the Matrix is a weird cage that we don't fit in — a manmade construct we've luckily escaped – at least from a workforce perspective, though we've still got some serious deconditioning to do. We've covered the fact that risk is an illusion, that humans over transactions are where it's at, and that you're gonna have to both *call out* AND *own your shit* if you're going to make it in business.

Now we have the thrilling (or terrifying? Same thing!) step of doing some honest-to-god actual entrepreneuring.

You and me, right here, right now.

Where are we starting? By digging in to get at your deeper why. You know, that big thing that your business exists in service of. And I'm not talking about the "I like to help people" level of why. I mean the deep shit. The stuff that you'll build your legacy work on.

This is what I like to call your *fingerprint* as a business owner. It's completely unique to you, and it's your greatest asset. It's also transferrable, so if you start a second business as I have, or a third or a fourth, your unique fingerprint is inherently a part of those businesses too. It's a combination of the ethics, values, and personal culture you bring into your work. And it's important because it's both impossible to compete with, and because it'll be a critical ever-present source of drive to keep putting your work into the world.

Illuminating this deeper why, this unique fingerprint, is one of the first crucial steps of being an entrepreneur that people tend to gloss over or just give a surface-level treatment and we're not going to do that here. We're going headlong into the inner work so that you're fortified for the slings and arrows that will inevitably come your way at some point or another.

[Insert panicked screaming.]

Yup. It's big. And it can be really intimidating when you don't have the first clue where to start. But here's the thing: you don't have to get it perfect. *You just have to do it.*

Why?

Because by engaging in this step you're going to be able to (1) build a more solid foundation for a viable, long-term business; (2) keep going through all the sleepless-night bits of entrepreneurship; and (3) avoid creating another job for yourself that you hate.

Pretty. Damn. Important.

The truth is that when we feel a disconnection from our work, or feel like it doesn't matter, it's because we've lost touch with the deeper why.

But don't stress. We're going to navigate this one together because it's important AF and I know the Force of the Incurables is strong in you.

It all starts with the why.

So, I run experience-delivery companies. They look like a business consultancy and a polar expedition company but really, at the root, they're delivering transformational experiences. This is important to me because it's what I love. I am crazy about customer service. I'm a stickler for details, for the little extras that delight. I'm an introvert who loves to connect with people in a controlled environment, and my businesses allow me to do just that.

My deeper why is that I want my work to be transformational in nature. By being an experience deliverer, I do just that with the people who come into contact with my work. Whenever work starts to feel like a bit of a toil, it's because I've gotten away from the heart of it. It's a great compass, a great reminder.

My deeper why is super resonant for me, and it's unique to me because of the points I listed above. My work is a direct extension of who I am as a human being and what gives me energy. It just happens to come in the form of consulting and running polar expeditions. The deeper meaning, combined with the unique-to-me format that it takes in how my work is delivered, truly encapsulates the person I am.

And as far as the deeper meaning, the experience deliverer in me keeps showing up in my work whether I like it or not. It's like I can't do business any other way.

"Don't give me a shitty pen."

Case in point: I'm obsessed with the details in my polar expedition company. Our guests pay an average of $10k per person for a 10-night trip on a small expedition ship with us. The kind of person who is willing and able to pay $10k for a 10-night trip isn't someone who's going to want a shitty pen in their cabin. No one has ever said, "Don't give me a shitty pen," but *I* don't want a shitty pen in my cabin when I travel so I'm not about to hand them out to our guests.

This means I have to spend quite a bit of time looking for a good-quality pen that we can brand with our company name and give out. Have you ever tried to source good pens that aren't obscenely expensive? It's fucking hard. Most pens are shitty. The ink doesn't flow well, or it flows too much and creates blobs. The pen is too thick or too thin to grasp easily, or its mechanism of action is annoying. (The twist vs. poke-top debate is real!)

I've had bags of sample pens sent to me and they're all crap. That's how obsessed I am with the details. I am not OK with giving my guests shitty pens. I want everything about their experience — from dealing with our office to travelling on our expeditions — to be high-end and well-thought-out. I want it all to feel delightful. It's one of the reasons I use the informal tagline in our newsletter, "Come as guests, leave as friends."

This shit matters. And I'm not putting it on. It *really* matters to me, because it matters to the people who take a chance on us and pay us good money for a unique travel experience.

The same can and should be true for an Internet-based service provider. Your end user should feel delighted and cared for. Don't give them shitty pens.

The challenge with virtual businesses is that it's easier to feel more disconnected from the end user than in a traditional business. In my expedition company, I meet all of the guests who sail with us because I fly up to the Arctic for the beginning of each trip and make sure everyone arrived OK and has all of their luggage, and I basically act as a company ambassador to see them all off on their epic adventure.

Whether we're selling direct to guests (in which case our office has direct contact with each paying client) or through a charterer (in which case we have no direct contact with the guests), either I or my team will be meeting these folks in person at the culmination of the business agreement. This makes everything feel much more real. While I like to think of myself and our staff as people of inherent integrity, the truth is that there's built-in accountability in the business model because we come face-to-face with the people who pay us to do what we do.

This isn't the case online. I've worked with clients and subcontractors in my online business for *years* and never met them in real life. People who you know online only are easier to perceive in the abstract. This is why we have boatloads of examples of shitty service providers who took your money and then ghosted you without finishing the project. Because you don't feel real to them. They got your money, and then some blockage happened or something with a higher priority came up so they abandoned your ship. You're just a person on the Internet that needed some graphic design. You're not tangible. Therefore, you got yourself some shitty pens.

Let me state this again: if you're building something that matters, something that will last, something that feeds you *and* adds value to others, your end user should feel delighted and cared for. Don't give them shitty pens.

And here's the really interesting thing: you'll often find that your business why is integrally connected with your deepest wants and needs.

I've realized over time that on a deeper level, the drive to create experiences that connect us is somewhat tied to me creating the village I never had. I don't have a family home — I don't even have a cohesive family! I'm not "from" somewhere because I moved around so much growing up, and I don't have people I can call up when I need help with something because I've never had the chance to set down roots of any kind until very, very recently.

So the deeper why of my work allows me to build businesses that affect others in meaningful, transformative ways. This creates a connection. This often creates affection, because people love it when you show through your actions that you really care. I never had that privilege before. But I've created an entrepreneurial environment that gives me the privilege to show that I care. To show that I see my clients and guests. And that their trust means something to me.

It's obvious that there's a deeper, more personal level of need there for me — which is awesome because it means that I get to create a proportionately deep response. If I hadn't had that wound from being untethered most of my life, I wouldn't have been able to create the cure.

Not that your deeper why has to be fixing some trauma or what have you. But digging in to uncover what you care about deeply, where the missing pieces are, that's what'll open the door to the legacy you're meant to create.

Unique Fingerprint Case Study: 100km Foods

What the business is: A local food distributor serving restaurants, retailers, and food businesses in Toronto and the Greater Toronto Area. Their mission is to establish a viable, dynamic, and sustainable local food economy whereby chefs have access to the freshest and best products that Ontario has to offer, and Ontario producers have a dedicated channel for the sales, marketing, and distribution of their products at a fair price.

What it really provides: A means for smaller growers and farmers to get their product to market with minimal middlemen skimming off their profit.

Their deeper why: Paul and Grace, the owners of 100km Foods, are driven by creating and testing more responsible forms of capitalism. They wanted a business that put the needs of all partners into the equation.

From the Founders

"100km Foods was created out of a desire for *meaningful* work. Work that aligned with our values; values of sustainability, fairness, equity, environmental conservation and damn good food. It was about doing things differently, bucking the status quo and creating new pathways, networks and connections that aimed to be *mutually beneficial to all parties involved*. Business done differently. Business as a force for good.

I very much value the work of non-profits, NGOs, charities etc. but these efforts are often fragile, precarious to shifts in the political zeitgeist, reliant on external funding sources. I firmly believe that *commercializing positive change* in the world can be a source of *lasting and permanent* change. With 100km Foods we are aiming to do just that, a for-profit business aimed at creating a lasting change in the food system, and impact the local economy in a synergistic mutually beneficial way for all parties involved, not the zero-sum formula that much of our traditional economy dictates.

After 12 years, we are immensely satisfied with the work that we do. I love getting out of bed in the morning. *I am proud to talk about what I do for a living.* It hasn't been all puppy dogs and rainbows. It's been fucking hard, brutal at times, but I wouldn't change it for the world."

Bringing it back together...

I guess it's getting pretty clear by now why you can't reverse engineer your deeper why from the outside in. It has to come from the inside out, because it's deeply tied to your identity and what matters to you the most. It's tied to the mark you want to make on the world based on your own strengths and value system.

And a great question to get deep into what that is for you is to ask yourself, *"What am I missing that I get to create via the medium of entrepreneurship?"*

The other half of the equation

Now it's time to look at the external implications of all this introspection. Because this book is about entrepreneurship, not navel-gazing! It's time to think about what effects you want to have through the work that you do. What legacy do you want to leave, long-term, in both the macro- and the micro-versions of your entrepreneurial world?

Making a difference (beyond profit)

Your end goal from a purely commercial perspective should always be to make more profit, which sounds really "dude-bro-y." But that's why we're in business. We're trying to be profitable without losing our heart.

But there's always a level beyond that, and most passionate entrepreneurs are interested in that next level. I heard 23andMe's founder Anne Wojcicki on a podcast the other day talking about how while it's natural that they created the service as a for-profit entity, the bigger-picture vision was to change the way people in the US could manage their healthcare, breaking down knowledge barriers and unnecessary costs for basic testing. When she ran into major roadblocks from the FDA, she saw it as an opportunity to *work with them* and change the face of consumer access to healthcare.

Through her drive to fix a system she could clearly see was broken, her company will ultimately gain in revenue. (Don't ever let them tell you that doing the right thing doesn't pay off!)

Another example: with Twin Tracks, we take people into the Arctic wilderness to see polar bears — an animal that may well become extinct within the next century — which is a pretty niche travel experience.

And because of where we begin our trips, guests have to fly far, and everybody knows that flying is the worst carbon footprint you can make as an individual. Therefore our industry gets a lot of flak from critics who question our claims that we operate as sustainably as possible.

My response? "Yeah we know our guests are leaving a carbon footprint, but there's no other way to do it." So, what do we do? How do we mitigate that?

The best way that we currently know how to combat our footprint is by having a carbon-offsetting program. The best way we can implement a carbon-offsetting program is by actually having carbon offsetting built into the fee for our trips. However, in order to carbon offset in a way that we can build it into the price like that is quite a costly ordeal for a tiny little company like ours.

Therefore, I'm extra motivated to *increase the revenue* in this company so that I can implement that program without noticing it in the financials at all. We want people travelling with us to feel like they made a really responsible decision aligned with their values that they don't need to feel guilty about.

Put simply, the more revenue you generate, the more impact you can have and the more empowered you are to make decisions that feel congruent with your ethics. Money doesn't buy freedom or time, but it buys options.

Making a difference is also about the effect that you, your work, and your company have on the people you interact with. No matter what you do or sell, your "thing" helps the buyer in some way. No matter whether you're a relationship therapist or a fancy-car salesperson, you're helping your end user become a better expression of themselves. And if you've built a business that allows you to do this in a way that's aligned with your ethics, then in more ways than one you're making a difference beyond profit.

The exception is if you're selling low-value crap and using NLP techniques to get people to purchase for fear of missing out. Unfortunately, the Internet business boom of the early 2010s was built on this. I mean really, how many times have you purchased a PDF or access to a webinar for a relatively low cost, but the return on your investment was similarly negligible? Those $99 products add up. You're lining the pockets of great marketers, but you're not adding real value to your own knowledge base. This is another reason to avoid the quick-fix promises, have patience, and build iteratively with a mind for serving your end user.

And lastly, the other way you can make a difference beyond profit (this one is probably my favourite) is that you can help the people you work with or who work for you. *You* can be the employer that pays fair living wages and builds other types of human-friendly policies into your contracts. You can be the person who promotes championing and advocacy amongst the people who work with or for you, creating an environment where people have creative license or autonomy that they may not have been able to find in the 9-to-5 world.

When your business does well, you can better afford to be generous. It becomes easier to be the person or the company that everyone loves to work with. And who doesn't want that?

When we started Twin Tracks, our team talked about the fact that even though we were tiny and not sure how soon we'd start turning a profit, we would always pay our guides very well — in the top percentile of wages — and we would always offer commission for referrals from friends in the industry (which is not a common practice). We also decided to buy excellent gear from the get-go, both expedition clothing of top rank as well as things like VHF radios, AED machines, and satellite phones. All of which is a *big* investment, but we wanted our staff to feel fully equipped and very well taken care of.

We do a myriad of other things for our guides and partners that are better than the industry standard and, as such, after only one season we had people knocking down our door asking for work.

The strategy is simple: treat people really well and you'll always stay ahead of the game. You'll always attract the best. You'll always be the first to be recommended. And then it becomes a cycle unto itself. Because of how we compensate our guides, we've enabled at least one staffer to quit taking contracts on bigger ships, work less, earn more, and spend a lot more time with his wife and baby back home. *That* is making a difference beyond profit.

Let's zoom out for a sec.

See how all this stuff is two sides of the same coin? The entire purpose of my businesses, the fingerprint of my work in the world, is to have meaningful interactions that move people forward. Externally, that translates to creating transformative experiences for my customers.

The external is a manifestation of the internal. I can only be good at what I do in my businesses because I'm so clear on the internal stuff. That's what keeps me clear and on track; it's the rubric by which I sort all my business decisions. What I'm trying to show you here is that knowing your why isn't *only* cool because of the mental clarity it gives you. It's also a necessary ingredient for creating the kind of business you want to run. And those experiences necessarily shape the next iteration of your internal stuff, and so on and so on, forever.

"Holy fuck, Heather, how can I conceivably know these things?"

Cue monkey brain dancing pantsless in your mind's eye trying to distract you with self-doubt and general WTF-am-I-looking-at-here sentiment.

Friend, *don't panic!*

I only have a certain degree of clarity around this deeper why shit for myself and my business because I've been working at it for 10 years.

All I want you to do right now is get to a *minimum viable why*.

You just need an inkling, a hint, to get started. Look for some sort of clue as to what energizes you, and what drains you. What kind of change do you want to be a part of? What injustice do you want to correct? Who needs to be included? What system is broken? What fucking matters anymore anyway?

And hey, remember that this process (like everything in entrepreneurship) is *iterative*. The whole point of being an entrepreneur is that you get ever closer and ever more nuanced with that why.

And *do not worry* about getting it perfect because it'll evolve and change, eventually getting to the point where you're bored with the version you have in front of you. And that's a great thing because guess what? You can change it!

That's entrepreneurship in a nutshell: create work that works for you, rather than the other way around. It's not about creating another job or locking yourself into another busy-work system. It's about moving that locus of control over your days from external factors to an internal devotion for the stuff that holds deep meaning for you.

NO PLAN B   **139**

No matter which way you slice it, you've gotta start somewhere.

Like I said earlier, look for the tiniest little first step. Hell, you can co-opt my why if that feels resonant. I don't care! We're usually copying other people in the early days anyway because it's all we know to work with.

And if you copy my why, the genius part is that you'll start to realize sooner or later that there are parts of it that don't feel right to you. And as long as you pay attention to those, adjusting away from the bleh and towards greater resonance, you'll be getting closer and closer to that big, clear fundamental legacy-level ride-or-die-motherfucker why. And that is rad.

Let's talk pitfalls...

Inevitably you're going to come up against pitfalls along your entrepreneurial journey because hey, if this were easy everyone would be doing it, right? It's important that we call these out early on so that when you experience them, you can recognize them for what they are and better navigate around them.

Pitfall 1: Paralysis

OK, so we've got all this big-picture stuff swirling around. Amazing. Inspiring, if not a wee bit terrifying as well. This is right about the time when you may start to feel a sort of mental paralysis set in. Then you'll be afraid to take action, and then just sort of fizzle.

I get it. People get super freaked out because they don't have all the answers. And so they're like, "Whoa, I don't know what to do here so I'm just not going to do anything."

And I'm here to tell you: just start. You *must* begin from where you're at. There is literally no other way. Like I said before, I don't care if you start with selling your backyard chickens' eggs. Just fucking start where you're at. There are no rules here. You just need to start running a business.

I started with an Etsy shop, then I stuck a basic website up and started coaching, then I tried group coaching, then I ran a few retreats, then this, then that, and and and. For a while I built low-budget websites on the side to supplement my income, and because I had to learn who I was as a business owner. I had to do a shitload of testing of ideas and of myself before I'd get things right. But the point is, I was never not taking action to move my income generation and my skill-building forward.

Put simply: there are the people that take action, and the people who do not. Full stop.

Which reminds me, you really have to not give a shit what anyone thinks because you're going to be iterating through phases of minimum viable service or product. And the first thing that comes up for most people is, "People will think XYZ of me. It's not going to look legit" or "I don't sound polished enough."

And to that I only have one response: who fucking cares? Now is the time to shed any concerns you have over other people's opinions. You're on a journey that will dramatically change your life, the lives of your loved ones, and potentially a much wider diaspora of people. You owe it to yourself to peel back the layers to get to your foundational why. You owe it to Future You! And the only way you can learn this is by doing it, by taking action. You cannot think your way into this type of clarity.

Pitfall 2: Getting a Personality Transplant

Pitfall #1 is paralysis, and pitfall #2 is trying to mimic someone successful.

Reader, do not do this. I know it's tempting, but people can smell a lack of originality 10,000 miles away. I saw a photographer post a photo on Instagram today of one of her clients with the caption, "Channeling her best Gabby Bernstein!" And you know what? She was! This woman looked, and dressed, and had hair like Gabby Bernstein!

Why. Why, why, why?!

It's like starting out as an actress and saying, "I want to be Meryl Streep" outta the gate. Yeah, right. You can't.

It sounds really simple when I lay it out like that...but people fall for it because we're sold the idea that what we see online is easily replicable or easily accessible for us. Or we assume that that level of success is just two years out if we work hard, and it rarely is. So you immediately set yourself up for failure if that's what you're trying to do. It's an easy trap to fall for because it looks like it's a blueprint. It looks like that's the thing you're supposed to aim for. That that's what you're supposed to emulate. Hell, it's sold as a blueprint by marketing experts and others of my ilk!

So, along those lines, Gabby Bernstein is really GD successful and people think if they model themselves after her, the masses will respond. But even if you get a little traction with this strategy, it will not last. I repeat, *it will not last*. Do you know anyone who is a semi-copy of someone else and is killin' it?

No. The successful entrepreneurs out there are all originals. You need to be an original too.

You can't become a better you by becoming a really good knock-off of someone else. It's not moving for your potential audience, nor for you. Mimicry is dead energy. It's like driving with the handbrake on.

Trying to be someone else is the opposite of motivating. It's the opposite of getting you going in the right direction and getting you as steeped in your craft as you need to be to do it really well.

It's like you're taking all of that amazing potential energy and putting it towards crafting this fake version of yourself instead of learning what the real version of you is and just being OK with that, whatever it is. Maybe you're not the most skilled businessperson right now. Fine. Whatever. Then it's your job to learn and get better, but you can't be a better you by trying to be a mediocre someone else.

Long story short: there is no blueprint of you. Which is *fucking amazing*.

Pitfall 3: Rushing It

You're stumbling into pitfall #3 when you try to rush it and go for something super polished right out the gate or pretend that you're more clear and "arrived" than you actually are.

You know...like when a business is clearly just one person but they keep using the word "we" in their web copy and represent themselves as a full agency.

Or when a business has a fairly polished website but the testimonials are from their mom's friend who they helped with their skills, or some random former work colleagues/bosses, and not based on the *actual* service that they're *currently* providing. Or even better, when they try to use a polished image (read: "I put this website and photoshoot on my credit card") as a jumping-off point for high-ticket items like masterminds but don't actually have the street cred and experience to support it.

Oh, or one of my very favourites, where you see someone who's a VA one month, a social media expert the next, a 'copywriting ninja' two months later, and then a business coach at the end of the year. There's nothing wrong with light reinvention, but pretending you're an expert at something you're still learning is problematic.

And, while you would never do this, some people do straight-up lie about their businesses and how successful they are, which is undeniably shitty.

I get why people do this — it's related to pride, and to the judgment of others. But when you pretend to be at a stage in business that you're not, you will inevitably fuck things up more than necessary. *Because you're not who you need to be for that stage yet.*

You can set yourself back years by starting with surface-level external focus. I'm not joking. I've seen "polished" businesses fold many times over because they skipped or glossed over the foundational internal stuff.

What you've got to do instead is look inward and get as clear as you can in this stage, and then create your minimum viable business from that place. Don't get me wrong — it doesn't need to look shitty. You can have a very polished external presence when you're starting out, but that can't be the only thing that's been given time and energy.

Rushing out of the gate will not make you more successful faster. It will more likely do the exact opposite. This isn't a race, it's a steady journey.

Pitfall 4: Accepting the boring

Entrepreneurship, for all its awesomeness, is inherently a little terrifying. I think we can all agree on this by now, yes?

So it makes sense that a lot of people would go into it and start looking for a new comfort zone.

Don't do it! It's a trap! Being a business owner is all about staying curious. It's all about running a series of experiments. It's about embracing the excitement of evolution. It's everything you ever wanted (never to be bored again!) when you were trapped in the 9-to-5.

I knew from the get-go that self-employment would never be a one-and-done scenario for me. I hated the atrophy of a j.o.b. So I started out with the starting-point why of "I want to help people" *and* I wanted better people skills. As such, I got my life coaching certification and I opened up a business as a life coach. And then I was like, "OK, so this is iteration one..." And after a while it felt too boring, too one dimensional.

Around this time, people were asking me, "How did you create a business online and move to Peru?" And I replied, "Well, I'll teach you." And so that become iteration two...which resonated a lot because I particularly like to help people build livelihoods that are outside of the Matrix.

Because deep down I'm a rebel. The first to scream and run from the traditional expectations of society. I've always felt that if I could lead my own revolution, I'd do it. And if that's what I get to do *with my work*, even better. Every little evolution of my business journey showed me more of what was possible. The evolutions peeled back more and more of the layers, and my business matured to get me to where I am now.

And that's going to change again!

A critical point to remember is that as an entrepreneur, you'll never *have arrived*. So the common line of inquiry of "needing to figure out what my one thing/passion is" has an inherent flaw because your one thing isn't one thing forever and ever, amen.

Just find out what your one thing is *right now*. And when you outgrow it, then you peel back the layers to find out what your one thing is at that next stage, and then your one thing gets more and more nuanced and more resonant and more magical and more powerful for you. And that — that process of never actually arriving at the final answer — is how you create this incredible legacy with your work. It's never being lazy about it.

You must be the type of person who isn't willing to (ever) accept the boring. Not just "I'm bored today" but the legit "I don't want to do life coaching anymore." The kind of boring that makes you want to stab yourself in the neck.

The whole point of getting out of the Matrix isn't so you can create another shitty job for yourself. It's so that when you get bored with life coaching or whatever variation you're currently in, you have the agency and motivation and insight into yourself to evolve into the next version of your work that's more closely aligned with who you have become. That's the whole point.

Pitfall 5: Giving a fuck what other people think

OK, so I'm not saying that you need to become some sort of anti-social asshole who never even gives a second thought to what other people think. But I can tell you that when you're doing this work, and figuring things out, you're going to be extremely vulnerable to social conditioning, naysayers, and well-intentioned people who have a certain idea of who you are and what your work is about but actually don't know anything.

You have got to learn to shut out what other people will think, what other people might say, and how people will judge your decisions. It's none of their business, and their opinions are none of your business!

This has to be like the most goddamn personal decision-making process and fact-finding internal mission that you have ever done. If there's ever a time to be true to yourself without the outside noise, it's now. I'm not gonna lie: the hardest thing you will ever have to do from an internal perspective is stay true to this. And that's exciting because that means that you're actually doing the work.

So what would it look like if you actually set aside other people's labels, just for a bit?

This is a great exercise for those of you who feel caught up in other people's judgments. What descriptors make sense for you? What labels have you been hiding behind that no longer represent who you've become? What descriptors are you afraid to say out loud for fear of judgment? For fear that you'll be seen as ungrateful for the opportunities you have in front of you that most people don't have? Or of being lumped in with "weirdos" or some kind of fringe movement...when in fact it's just who you are?

It's a bit scary, I know. So I'll start.

Hi, I'm Heather. I'm an atheist and kind of a hermit.

I also hate being serious and love telling jokes at parties, on the rare occasion I go to a party. I'm exceptionally light-hearted but I also get really fired up (my husband would call it angry) when I witness things that are backward, inefficient, or unfair. Despite being an introvert and an atheist, I'm not a weirdo who can't handle people or church. I'm one of those people who can have a conversation with almost anyone because I grew up all over the world so I can always find a point of connection. And I have friends of every faith you can imagine. But parts of my core identity are atheism and hermitude. And those two elements directly inform not only my life choices, but also how I run my business and who I align myself with.

What does that look like in action? Well, for starters my secular approach to life acts as a signal to people of faith that I might not be a good fit for them as a coach. For example, I state on my website under the Who This Is Not For section that "If thoughts and prayers are your jam, I might not be the coach for you." I share publicly that my approach to business and life is through the lens of reason and science. Will this turn some people off? Absolutely! And that's great. That's the point. I am not for everyone.

My hermitude? It means that I'll rarely (rarely) agree to meet up with people just for the heck of it. I've had a number of people let me know they're passing through Sweden and it would be great to meet up, but it takes a lot...I can't even tell you how much...for me to actually get on a train or in the car and come to meet up somewhere. (I mentioned I live in the boonies, right?) I don't like hanging out. I abhor small talk. I don't need company. Please don't invite me to your Christmas party. It's a 9/10 that I won't come.

But here's an important bit: it's not that I don't like people, or don't appreciate interactions with humans in other ways. I really love and am grateful for a lot of the friendships and connections I've made online. In fact, I would say they're critical for my mental health. Like I said earlier, it's why I'm developing an online community, as a surrogate for the proverbial village we've lost, in large part so that people like me who are just honest-to-god card-carrying introverts can feel like they belong to a group of kindred, helpful friends without having to do the thing that drains the shit outta them (like meet up in person). Ain't nothing wrong with that. And there ain't nothing wrong with you for not wanting to socialize.

My point is that we shouldn't be afraid of being who we really are. *Of claiming who we have been all along.*

You probably moved through parallel phases in life, dealing with your own shit and figuring out your own uniqueness. You may still be moving through it. But in the end, only you know the real you and can understand both the conditions you need to thrive and why.

Find it, own it, and never apologize for it.

The funny thing is, in the context of entrepreneurship, if you keep your eyes on your own paper and stop caring what other people think, like I do, *it doesn't make any difference.* Nobody's sitting there thinking, "Oh, you're selfish and rude for not listening to my opinion." You know? Rather, you'll find most people say,

"Wow, you're so inspiring."
"You're so independent."
"You're so fearless."
"I could never do that!"

If anything, being true to yourself is something that we exalt.

So, head down. Eyes on your own paper. Pull that minimum viable why together for the stage that you're at from your internal cues, because it's incredibly personal. You've already taken the first step by reading this chapter, so it's mostly downhill from here.

Congrats on making it through a mofo of a chapter! This is big, important work. And it's a big deal that you're willing to take the time and the discomfort to go through it.

Gone are the days of flailing along and listening to the bullshit on the Internet. This is your thing. You are an incurable entrepreneur, and you need to go into this eyes wide open. Doing this work will set you up so much better in the long run. You'll be so much stronger and faster than you would be if you didn't embrace this process.

Yes, it takes time, and it's a pain in the ass, but you're tilling the fields deep and Future You will thank you for it. The good news is that the next few chapters are going to be fun — we're talking cognitive loads, becoming a master decision-maker, and learning how to game your system.

Understanding Your Cognitive Load (aka You Do Not Suck)

RIGHT-O, WE'RE DONE WITH the fluffy bits for a while because there's only so much introspection we can indulge in before we have to actually put the hammer to the nail. You know...strike while the iron's hot and all those great metalsmithing analogies.

Time for more concrete mental management tools and less "What's the fingerprint of your soul..." *(Whew, right?)*

Because really, that's what you're here for. That's what *I'm* here for. Look, you do have to know thyself in order to do great work. So there's a place for all the bits I just walked you through. But a lot of people get stuck there and I've always been a shit-or-get-off-the-pot kinda chick. We're action takers! Not quite productivity hackers, but definitely not naval gazers either. There is a happy, healthy medium that will require a *lot* of you, but still be manageable.

In this chapter, we're going to start talking about how you can act on your why over time in a way that doesn't leave you burnt out and hating life. And a big foundational part of that is understanding your cognitive load, aka how many plates you can juggle at one time without wanting to cry.

The lay of the (4-hour work week) land

Cue the ubiquitous narrative that became a "thing" around 2010, that the ultimate #lifegoal is to work as little as possible, preferably from a beach in Thailand, and make the Internet your new cash machine by setting up systems that ram unsuspecting dreamers into your paid product funnels. That's modern entrepreneurship, folks! At least it is according to the dude-bro entrepreneurs who promise a lifestyle of minimal responsibility and, thusly, minimal cognitive load.

I mean, gahddamb...how sexy is that idea? You can work so little and just enjoy life spacing out in your own personal version of *The Beach*? (Hint: *That* didn't end well, did it, DiCaprio?)

It's really important to remember that most of entrepreneurship, most of the *journey of entrepreneurship*, is a constant act of getting over yourself. It's not *hard*, per se. As in, you don't wake up every day and think, "Oh, I'm in pain!" But it's not *easy*.

Here's the thing: go look at the example of nearly every founder of every small to medium company since 2001 about what the fuck it takes to build a company. Yes, someday, if you're smart, and if you learn how to delegate, and if you learn how to make good decisions, and if you're a generous leader and a generous manager, and if you stay true to your vision, you'll eventually be able to rest on your laurels. But everything else you hear on the Internet about "making six figures by Christmas" is largely bullshit.

Look, everybody that you see right now that's high-profile enough
to have a recognized business spent a good decade building up their
reputation before anybody knew who the hell they were, you know?
Everybody: Marie Forleo, Jim Kwik, Danielle LaPorte, Ramit Sethi,
Jonathan Fields. Take Jonathan's Good Life Project. He did *loads* of
things prior, including working as a yoga teacher and running Career
Renegade. The GLP is just his latest iteration. He put in the time to
learn how to be strategic and good at what he does, which is what
allowed him to launch the Good Life Project to such success.

Brené Brown is another good example. People think she just fell out
of the sky and did a TED Talk and then blew up in popularity. Nope,
sorry. Brené Brown had been working her buns off as a professor
and researcher for about two decades before it culminated in her
monumental book, *Daring Greatly*, which she's now leveraged to grow
a bigger platform.

Long story short: people who get into this gig to only work 12 hours a
week don't impress me.

We're not trying to be successful just to make money just so we can
live free and easy. We're on a bigger mission. And frankly, the four-
hour work week thing as understood by the dude-bros sounds like
something I would do if I had given up, you know?

The people reading this book are ambitious and want to use their
talents to build things that have reach beyond themselves. We're not
about minimizing cognitive load to the point of making the Internet
an ATM. We're about using entrepreneurship as a medium to deliver
whatever our unique contribution is. Which often leads people to...

**The opposite blessing/curse: wanting to do all the things all
the time.**

Congratulations! You're not a dude-bro entrepreneur looking to automate your business so far to the fringe that you barely need to think about it. (#notpossibleanyway) Hooray! You're wired up and ready to go! And let me tell you, it is SUPER cool to be a part of a community of incurable entrepreneurs who are up to great, world-shifting things.

But now you've got to get comfortable with being in a steady state of figuring things out. Your to-do list is a giant mish-mash of answers to be hunted down for yourself or your business. This is especially true when you're *growing* the business because you've never grown that business before! It's a constant process of getting over yourself, getting over your own hangups, getting over your own resistance, and getting over your own procrastination.

And that is why it's critical that you're feeling fired up right now. That's awesome! You should be. If you weren't, I'd be worried. Because we have tough work to do, and the tough bits aren't going to last, but you'll need the extra oomph to navigate these next steps.

Enter the next major pitfall of entrepreneurship: how being so ambitious and excited can come back to bite you, because most of the time things aren't going to be exciting, per se. They're going to be mildly overwhelming. Most of the journey is the relentless art of getting over yourself, again, and again, and again. And as I mentioned before, it's not hard in the "painful" sense, but in the "becoming something new" sense.

Of course, you *can* dive in and try to ride the wave of enthusiasm forever, like most people do, but then you'll find yourself in another trap of being busy all the time, not having the right processes in place, not having pricing that takes into account labour costs, etc. etc. etc. In other words, you'll be stuck in employee mode, even if you're the boss of you. This is a fast track to burning out and hating your business.

You are the primary resource driving your business, so it's of critical importance that you take care of yourself physically, mentally, and financially. For example, a regular issue with a lot of freelancers is that they don't price themselves properly and they end up struggling for enough money to get by, let alone grow their business. Then they start trying to attract clients from a place of scarcity, often convincing themselves, "Oh, I know this client isn't the right fit, but it's an extra five hundred bucks in my pocket which I really need right now." I promise you that these decisions cause more trouble than they're worth. Therefore starting with the personal — your basic physical, mental, and financial needs — is key.

Because here's the deal: *passion is not a sustainable resource.*

You don't want to escape the cage of a job in order to put yourself into another type of trap. We all know what it feels like when you have so much on your plate that not only do you not know where to begin, but you also just feel like, "I'm done. This isn't worth it." That feeling of "You could stick hot pokers in my eyes and I'm still not going to want to start dealing with what I need to deal with. I know this is what I need to do to run my business, but I've just burned through my motivation."

I think we've all been there at some point, at different stages of building a business. You're just sitting there going, "I've got nothing." Because you haven't yet gotten to that place where you're self-managing properly or delegating properly or triaging what's important properly and just not fucking doing some of the stuff that you think you should be doing because often that's a big piece of it. Right? We have all things in our headspace that keep us in a constant running dialogue of, "I've gotta do this, I've gotta do that, and I keep meaning to start posting regularly on LinkedIn but I'm still not doing it."

As we talked about earlier, you and I aren't just in this for the money. We're impact making and ecosystem shifting with our work. So when the chips are down, you've got to remember why you're here to begin with.

You have to care about the mission enough to preserve the most important resource in the mission: yourself.

It's easy to feel shame when you get into that state of being overwhelmed (because it will probably happen, even if you try to set yourself up for it not to happen). You're not *that person*, right? It's not in line with the story you tell yourself.

But the story you tell yourself about how capable you are needs to take a seat. Your ego is not what's important here. What's important is that you take a breather. Get a night of good sleep. And then you use the tools that I'm sharing in this book and plug back into the meaningful bits of your work. Take the time to orient yourself so that you have the headspace to re-engage and create the boundaries required for the breathing space you need to keep going with the mission, you know?

I know you want to lie down and rest for a long-ass hiatus while someone else does the work for you but actually, you have to guide the process of growing your business. You don't have to do all the things yourself, but you still have to be in charge of the mission, which means you can't check out completely when you're feeling burned out.

So, find an anchor to always return to as your baseline. For me, it's *"You're the one you've been waiting for."* Find something to inspire you to keep going. To remind you of the critical importance you place on autonomy or creativity or never returning to *the way things were*. Take a moment to quiet your mind and listen to the first thing that comes up for you...the anchor you need to keep going when the going gets rough.

Write it down. Stick it up in your workspace. Make it the background on your laptop. Whatever works. Your anchor is as important as your unique fingerprint. It needs to be front and center.

What comes next? Well, a few things...like understanding your cognitive load, learning how to game your system, and mastering some technical things like decision-making.

Introducing cognitive load

I'm leading here with cognitive load because it's a critical piece of self-management that most of us who've come from the working world kind of suck at in the beginning.

As a small business owner you need to ensure you don't spread yourself too thin, not only because of burnout but because *you are the holder of the business vision* and you need to retain perspective on the critical elements of your business. The bad news is that as someone with a human brain, you can't retain perspective when you're strung out and overwhelmed, so the way that you avoid being strung out and overwhelmed starts with understanding your cognitive load.

Cognitive load, technically speaking, is the total amount of mental activity imposed on working memory in any one instant. But in the context of entrepreneurship, I think of it as how many things you're juggling at any given time in your own brain, and more importantly, how much of it you're taking on the responsibility for. Another way of looking at it is that cognitive load is essentially the cards you have to play with. It's your energy, the units of attention, the spoons you've got to give in any given situation.[4]

So if you feel responsible for, let's say, 50 working pieces in your business, and you're maxed out, that's not good. That's the thing about cognitive load. It's the reason it's a "load." The word itself insinuates a heaviness on you because of the responsibility. It's in your mind. It's on your shoulders. If you don't do it, there will be some kind of negative outcome, or a perceived missing out, or a lost opportunity.

And what if you get that out of your head and onto paper or onto someone else's plate? It lightens your cognitive load because it's no longer in your brain, no longer your responsibility. It's no longer the *weight you have to bear.*

If left unchecked, your cognitive load can easily snowball because running a business has a lot of moving parts. You must start early by keeping your finger on the pulse, recognizing the cues, and being protective of your own headspace as you prioritize and delegate.

If you're always operating on that razor's edge of almost being maxed out (as so many incurables do), then what happens when a wrench gets chucked in the works? What happens in a time of crisis or unexpected interruption that needs your full attention? Burnout city, my friend. Don't go there.

To be responsible for ourselves and our well-being outside the Matrix, we must have our eyes wide open and see the potholes in front of us so we can work to avoid them.

---

4 This is totally unscientific; I'm not a scientist, I'm just leveraging existing terminology and applying it to the experiences we have as business owners.

How to figure out what your cognitive load is

Recognizing your maximum cognitive load is understanding that point at which you start to feel too busy.

This is probably different for everyone, but for me one major indicator is when I start to feel almost a low-level anxiety. It's when my cortisol starts kicking in before the sun rises. It's when I start thinking, "Wow, I've woken up three days in a row at 5 a.m." I know what that is.

(That internal voice that many of us have shouting, "Whatever! I can do all the things!" is such a blessing and a curse, isn't it?)

So your job here is to learn what your cues are. It may be as simple as starting to feel too busy. But what does "too busy" mean? Be specific:

Are you starting to dread certain tasks?
Are things that used to be easy really draining for you now?
Are you starting to forgo things that you used to do as "free time" activities?
Are you not going for your daily walk because you've just got too much going on?
Have you got cortisol pumping through your brain at 5 a.m. like I have?
Do you have too many browser tabs open — literally on your laptop and figuratively in your brain — that are slowing your system down?

No two incurables are the same, but for me, those are the cues that I'm exceeding my maximum cognitive load and they don't feel good. Those signs are when I know I'm starting to go down a slippery slope. That's when I have to be a little bit more ruthless with my decision-making. It's when I've got to Chuck Norris some shit 'round here. Either I have to *not* do certain things at all, or I have to say no a little bit more, or I have to look at whatever it is that's weighing on me and just make an executive decision.

Yes, even if it's a good idea that might help the business. Even if I have this grand plan to start showing up three times a week on LinkedIn. If there are other things that are more pressing and that small item is weighing on me unnecessarily, I'm going to *parking lot* that shit and I'm not going to think about it until Christmas.

My business isn't going to fold if I don't start doing that thing, you know what I mean? It's *that* decision-making. It's *that* prioritizing around things that may not be critical and are rather just busy work in the current landscape of my daily deliverables.

And sometimes it's just saying, "I had every intention to do this, but I've changed my mind because right now the capacity isn't there. It's getting delayed until further notice and it's not in my headspace. It's not going to be part of my cognitive load right now because I'm going into the unhealthy zone."

How it's going to change over time, both in capacity and management

The wonderful thing about your cognitive load is that it's going to change over time. In the beginning, a hell of a lot of your bandwidth is going to be allocated to figuring out who you are as an entrepreneur. When everything is new, it's a zillion times harder and more draining to figure out, even if it's something stupid like figuring out how to put a favicon on your website. It's new, so it takes more bandwidth, even if it's not "hard."

But like anything new, it'll then become part of your repertoire and your headspace will open up to new things. You'll have more capacity because you will have built it, like a muscle.

These days, I can have shit majorly hit the fan and still be OK, because I've spent years building the capacity to handle it. And, importantly, I don't hold any judgment about it. Things are what they are, I'm not going to beat myself up over it. Why shit on myself when I'm actually doing the best that I can?

I mean, I'm not lazy. If I were lazy or didn't pay attention to innumerable important things, then maybe I should be wagging my finger at myself on occasion. But I believe that most people who are very ambitious, driven, and mission-oriented (like you and me) are not lazy. We're not trying half-assed. We're not making silly mistakes, you know, so let's get that fucking judgment out of there.

It goes back to that story I tell about making a very conscientious decision to put down a deposit on that polar trip that we later had to cancel in our first season. My internal dialogue was crystal clear: "I'm making this payment understanding I might lose a huge chunk of my own savings. I'm making this decision based on the best data that I have right now. I believe in myself, I believe in the data, I believe in our ability to pull this off." And then when I lost the money I was like, "Oh, fuck."

Of course I was bummed out.
Of course I had a shitty day.

But it wasn't like, "You fucking stupid idiot. What were you thinking?" There was no beating myself up because I made the decision from the right place. And you learn from that. Right? You're fine. I was fine. Everyone's fine. Let's move on.

Then we had this situation in our 2019 season where we had to cancel a charter due to a ship malfunction from a rogue fishing net getting caught in the propeller shaft. A company member who is

NO PLAN B   161

not entrepreneurial said, "Well, now we're screwed. We should just close up shop." And my response was, "Why? We haven't actually lost anything. The charter is being moved to a future season. We haven't lost any business. We're cool. We're doing an amazing job. This company is really something to be proud of. This actually has nothing to do with us. A fishing net has zero to do with us. Shit happens."

It would be easy to get overloaded in a crisis scenario, especially when you put in years (even one or two!) of hard work and development to get to where you're at. *The real killer isn't the maxing out of your cognitive load, it's the judgment and criticism that comes from the inside when things don't go well.* We are quick to blame ourselves when our tanks are low and we're running on fumes. But this doesn't help at all.

In fact, whenever I feel I'm facing a less-than-stellar situation, rather than giving in to the fear, anxiety, or negativity that desperately wants to take the wheel, I let logic and solution-thinking help me manage my cognitive load. I decide on my emotional response, which is to look at the data in front of me and ask, "What will be useful and helpful right now?" (Hint: hand-wringing, cold towels on the forehead, and ominous proclamations are a colossal waste of time.)

If you remember nothing else from this chapter, remember that removing judgment and criticism is a key part of cognitive load management.

Everything changes all the time — and that's OK.

As an entrepreneur, you're choosing to be in a constant state of fluctuating needs and priorities. People tend to get really hung up on that. As in, they make the plan, and then they get frustrated when they can't follow through on it in exactly the way they thought they would, and they feel like they've failed.

But the reality is that we use different tools over time to achieve the success that we want. Right? As I said before: there's no one thing that's going to make or break your business. In this day and age it's not so cut and dry, especially if you're a solopreneur or an online entrepreneur.

It's not like that *one* strategy or that *one* tactic you were planning on implementing will harm your business because you've put it off. Who farking cares, you know? We need to not be so attached to "I said I was going to do this" or "I said I'd do that."

You had some intentions, then life happened, and those intentions got shuffled and that's cool. This is your umpteenth reminder to constantly remove judgment from your situation.

What this is *not* is a get-out-of-jail-free card to be a flake or a dick about deliverables to others.

It's really important for you to be able to show up every day and coexist with the fluctuating needs and priorities of your business. Because the alternative, the beating up of self...the sitting around stuffing your face with popcorn and watching Netflix instead of Doing the Work...that's because you're running from judgment. You don't want to face your own judgment of yourself.

A lot of times a client will show up to a call and say, "I didn't do half the stuff I said I was going to do last month because because because because because..." and I'm like, "Cool. OK. Let's talk about what just needs to be Chuck Norrised." No need to be sentimental. Let's just prioritize and get down to brass tacks.

This is just part of the dance of entrepreneurship and capacity management. It's a constant readjustment of priorities. Downsizing, prioritizing, changing your mind, reframing the concept of "failure." It's shifting in the name of what's best for the business and what makes sense for your cognitive load.

I'm sure you're wondering how on earth one can run a business if you're constantly shuffling things and changing your mind. The beauty of it is that you can make these constant shifts, and manage your capacity in this way, while still knowing that you're moving in the right direction because you've got that fingerprint — that why, the big reason — to keep coming back to. As long as where you're focusing your energy serves that, you're all good.

It's all starting to make sense now, right? And here you thought I was just making you figure that big why stuff out first because I'm cruel or secretly woo-woo. (Ha!) But actually, it was entirely logical, designed so that you could get to this part — this zone of constant fluctuation which makes or breaks most people — and have that foundation to lean on.

What to do if you're in crisis

Since I'm not a lying liar, I've gotta break it to you that even the most adept energy managers are sometimes going to be just way fucking above capacity. Things are going to go to shit. You're going to feel exhausted and burnt out and like you don't have any more fucks to give.

It happens, and it's nothing to be ashamed of. Life is full of unpredictable scenarios and you know what they say about best-laid plans. Again, the whole point is that we learn to use situations we find ourselves in as *information* — as data points — not an excuse to beat up on ourselves. Remember that you're relatively new to this, even if you've been in business for a few years, because we've all been socialized to follow other people's instructions when it comes to work. You're making the leap from a framework (and expectations) you've been steeped in for the first 20 (or more) years of your life to something that has no structure at all. It's a whole different game.

So when the shit hits the fan, please start with being gentle on yourself. Don't allow the shame to creep in. It's not useful, nor necessary, nor warranted. We all go through the same slings and arrows at some point in our entrepreneurial journey and the only thing you can control is how you react. Take a breather, get some sleep, and use the tools I'm about to run through to move forward.

How to get out of a crisis (big or small, it doesn't matter)

Begin with a reset.

First, step away for 24 hours. Me? I take some time to physically get out of my work zone (which is my house because I work from home) and I go to the forest.

Then get a good night's sleep because oh my god, that is the best thing ever. Reset your clock. And then come back to your business with a clear, fresh mind. *Do not underestimate the power of these two steps!!* They literally take the edge off nearly every problem, ever.

Next?

You get to start karate chopping stuff and narrow your daily deliverables down to three priority items. You're going to have to be cutthroat here because when you're super overwhelmed you *must* parking lot or get rid of items that simply aren't critical. Nothing is more important than your mental health and capacity to do what matters in your business. And you know what? Only a handful of things really matter.

But what if you don't know what matters? (I hear you!)

One of the reasons we feel overwhelmed is because what's before us feels so nebulous. Everything on your to-do list *feels important*. It feels big and unruly. Sometimes it's super hard to know where to start so you just get paralyzed and then don't make any progress.

Enter: baby steps. Break that shit down, friend. Ask yourself, "What's one action that I can take to start moving towards resolving this?"

For example, if you don't know where to start with your business taxes, what's step one? What's the very first thing you have to do? Get on top of your bookkeeping? OK, go in and print out your credit card statements and start knocking off each thing on your statement and finding the invoice. Just do that. Just start there. Because that's the only way forward, right?

Got a bigger issue? When you're overwhelmed, being inside your own brain is the worst place to be. So get out of it. Talk to someone about the things you're grappling with and have them ask the micro-questions that will help you break things down and find the path of least resistance.

Now you'll start moving through the things that felt super difficult before and you're going to feel like you can breathe again. Once you feel back on track and you've got a few of those big ugly things out of the way and you're thinking, "That was a lot easier than I thought," then you can start bringing back in the non-urgent things, the non-critical things, and move into the "OK, now I can get back to my regular posting on Instagram" stage.

When you're buried under Things That Need to Get Done the point is to recognize that nobody's died. Nobody's lost a limb.

Your business isn't going to fold.
You need a hug.
You need a good sleep.
You need to go outside.
And then you go from there.

Whew! I hope this chapter helped you feel like self-management and resilience are totally achievable. I promise they are. It just takes practice and a whole lotta self-compassion.

Soft skills *sound* easy, but this transition is one of the fucking hardest things you'll ever have to do. You're evolving. Building the habits of working for yourself. Building the skills of an incurable entrepreneur.

So hey, take it easy on yourself. The curve is steep.

Everybody says, "You don't know how hard it is to be a parent. You have no idea what to do. You don't know how to successfully keep the child alive."

This is no different.

You're embracing a new identity, which is totally rad, and I'm going to help get you there.

In the very next chapter, I'm going to walk you through some skills that will help make things easier.

Next up? Gaming your system.

Gaming Your System

THIS IS PERHAPS ONE OF the most important sections of this book if you ever want to ship work that matters. For the purposes of this explanation, I'm going to assume that if you're reading this you're (a) somewhat of a multi-passionate type and (b) do not have a trust fund you can lean on.

Here's the deal: work that matters requires us to consistently show up. Maybe you need to show up every day and write (like I am right now) to ship your book. Maybe you need to post promos for your business three days a week on social to generate new leads and maintain authority in your sphere. Maybe you need to be consistently available for your team to make executive decisions on things. No matter the situation, your work needs you.

The problem? Every Fucking Thing that gets in the way. Mostly procrastination. I read recently that some of the most successful visionaries are the worst procrastinators and I believe it. But also things like depression — a *huge* issue in the entrepreneurial world which can kick your motivation right in the ballsack on any given day without warning. And lifestyle too. Because let's face it, in this day and age of people running online businesses and holding non-traditional work hours, the simple day-to-day stuff of life can get in the way.

Procrastination, unconventional work hours, odd workspaces (cafes, ships in Antarctica), feeling massive resistance towards certain business activities that really need to get done...it's like being Super Mario trying to save Princess Peach and having every obstacle imaginable being tossed in your path.

But none of this is an excuse to not do the work. So, I'm going to throw down the one strategy that has worked for me consistently for years and it requires some fancy footwork. But in the end it's the same concept, repeated based on circumstances:

Gaming your system.

Call it a productivity hack, whatever. (I'm not a fan of that term as it insinuates productivity for productivity's sake. And productivity means nothing if the work is pointless.) What does "gaming your system" mean anyway? And when should you employ this superpower?

It means whenever you come up against roadblocks in your work, you find a creative way to remove that block. Trick yourself. Ask yourself how you can make this seemingly daunting task wildly doable. Most of the time this is nothing more than breaking larger projects into the tiniest baby steps, but sometimes it means using a software that makes things easier. Or asking someone for a second set of eyes, or hands, on something you've been working on.

Here's an example of a resistance pickle I'm in right now. Up until two days ago, I'd hardly written a thing for a whole month. I'm *supposed* to be writing content for this book every day. But I've been doing... nuthin'. I managed to bang out about 5,000 words on an airplane to Canada, but that's because everyone else was sleeping, it was dark, I had no Internet, I'd cleaned out my entire hard drive and organized my desktop (ha!), and there was nothing else to do but motherfucking *write*. But after that burst, nuthin'.

And it's not like I don't want to write this book. I want to write this book more than anything. But...resistance! I can't explain it. I don't need to analyze it. It's just there. Being annoying. Stopping me from producing my ideas and pouring them onto paper.

"Oh, hai."

So when I had a call with my editor two days ago I said, "Look, telling you I'm going to write won't work. And while general accountability doesn't usually work for me, I want to break this down and tell you that (a) I'm going to commit to writing 500 words a day for 20 days, (b) I'm going to email you every second day to report that it's done, and (c) I'm going to schedule one hour each day in my calendar as non-negotiable time to make sure it happens." Because I can do anything for 20 days, especially when it's only writing 500 words. That's 100% DOABLE.

System = gamed.

I know I won't fail because 20 days is about my maximum of sticking to something that's out of my usual routine.

Here's one thing you should never do. (Yup, I'm making a blanket "should never" statement because it's *important*.) Never, ever, ever beat yourself up or give yourself any kind of grief whatsoever because you didn't follow through on something that's important to you.

This shit is HARD. Anything worth doing is hard. Motivation doesn't magically occur 99% of the time for *anyone*. Yes, it can feel like you've been shot out of a cannon of inspiration when you start a project or a new business endeavour. But that never lasts. Never, ever, ever, ever. So why would you internalize procrastination or lack of motivation as some kind of character flaw? Son, it has nothing to do with you. Zero. Nada. Got it? Good.

The truth is that people who are "successful" don't have some special superpower you don't have. They don't know a secret that people who struggle aren't aware of. They aren't more motivated or focused. *They don't want it more than you.*

Don't listen to those assholes who tell you if you haven't achieved X yet it's because you don't want it bad enough. Or you're not trying hard enough.

They ALL feel resistance.

They ALL procrastinate, likely just as much as you do.

They ALL stare at their computer screens or their running shoes by the door or their guitar against the wall — whatever medium they rely on to achieve the thing that takes their aspirations to the next level — and feel blank sometimes. Often, even.

Take away the people with family money to equalize the playing field, and the most successful people are no different from you.

The key is in looking at resistance or obstacles and changing your approach.

It's worth taking a moment to address the ever-ubiquitous dude-

bro "just fucking do it" rally cry that we see on the interwebs.
When you try to implement that mantra, you set yourself up for
failure because you're taking psychology out of the mix. We're not
bulldozers. And we're not one-dimensional beings. We're extremely
complicated beings!

We have fears and anxieties and knowledge gaps and financial gaps
and varying degrees of cognitive load capacity, among a million other
factors. We all have different amounts of time available to us, based
on our life circumstances, to build the things we believe in. Not to
mention widely differing energy levels. This mantra of "just fucking
do it" is, in my view, a precursor to feeling ashamed and unworthy.
Because it's not in any way a human-friendly nor realistic approach to
building a business sustainably.

Yes, it takes a lot of hard work. But that Gary Vee–level sleep-when-
you're-dead, your-real-friends-will-stick-around-even-if-you're-too-
busy-crushin'-it-to-be-a-good-friend business approach? Nah. I'll take
a hard pass, thanks.

So, back to the inevitable obstacles...

Your *only* job is to do what it takes to find a way around, over, or under
those motherlovers. They will never go away. But you can be Super
Mario and leap around them. You can jump right on top of them. You
can sneak under them. You must!

It's the only way.

I *really* encourage you to develop this skill of gaming your system.
Find tools to remove the resistance. Call in for reinforcements when
necessary. And recognize that your fix might only work for a short
time. That's cool too. I know that my 20-day accountability marathon

with my editor won't work beyond that 20 days. In other words, it works precisely *because* it's only 20 days. I can do anything for 20 days!

What works to get ideas out of me and onto this screen right now might not work next month or next year, so I have to keep iterating. I have to keep asking myself: what's most important and what do I need to make it happen right now? And I usually have multiple gamification strategies happening at once for all different elements of my two businesses. That way I'm spending 20 minutes here, an hour over there, changing up my left-brain work to right-brain stuff and keeping things interesting and fresh. Find different ways. Resistance is nothing more than a speedbump.[5]

Long story short: you have to game your system to be the person you need to be to run the business you want to run.

Of course, there's a lot more to bringing your great work to life beyond gaming your system, but this is a non-negotiable piece of the puzzle.

If you've ever read any books by the big guns like Richard Branson, they are full of tales of how they've gamed their systems or, in other words, got around obstacles that were fundamental parts of who they are (and therefore not likely to change). Branson himself is dyslexic and talks openly about how he's used delegation right from the beginning to help propel his ideas forward.

And I know you might be thinking that you don't have the resources,

---

5 PRO TIP: If you haven't read it (or even heard of it), get thee to a place where you can borrow or buy books and find Steven Pressfield's *The War of Art*. It is one of the best books I've ever read, for any human, to be better at being a human. *The War of Art* is 190 pages of absolute brilliance and will help you immeasurably with your relationship to resistance.

etc. etc. etc. But I'm going to stop you right there. Because what we're talking about here is fundamentally an inside job. You must believe you can find the solution, and feel that your ideas and mission are worthy of it, before you can make it happen.

Put simply: there is always a solution. And this chapter is going to prime you to be the kind of person who makes the seemingly impossible possible.

Grab a pen for notes because I'm going to talk about the six main areas you really need to delve into and learn to game.

Confidence

Confidence is probably the single most important ingredient in actually shipping your work. If you're not confident, you're much less likely to show up. Even more accurately, you will not show up in the way *that you need to show up*. You might physically be there, but you may as well be an ironing board with a top hat.

Without confidence, you've got little to work with. Your toolbox is locked.

Here's the thing: we've all experienced the smoke and mirrors of someone who portrayed themselves one way but completely didn't live up to that in reality. You might have all the right ingredients on the surface, but without true confidence backing it up, the foundation is faulty. We're talking Swiss cheese here. You're gonna fall through one of those holes in the floor when the tiniest breeze hits.

I used to know a woman from an online course I took. She looked like a total badass online. And I mean...super badass. Confident, fashionable, thin and cute, a great backstory, *on top of her game and winning at life.* I was admittedly a little envious. I wished I had her polished business-coach vibe and thought, "She's someone whose star is going to rise. She's got this digital business thing *down.*"

But when I met her in person she was so insecure that her body language made it look like she was about to shrink into herself. Fast forward a few years and she's primarily working for someone else. She still has a website up and blogs sporadically, but she's nothing like the powerhouse online maven that she sold herself to be in the early days.

I want to make it clear that this isn't a judgment call on her. She's one of the thousands living the exact same story. She's not even necessarily bad at what she does. The problem is that living that kind of "fake it 'til you make it" lie when it comes to confidence takes *so* much energy that it's not sustainable. Not to mention it must be a horrible burden to live with the feeling that you're going to be found out. And the reality is that if you're crippled, you cripple the business.

You need all your energy for actual business building, not maintaining a painfully false image.

So we're not going to let that happen to you. Let's delve into some proven age-old wisdom that's going to help you game your system to become the confident person you need to be.

First off, stop paying any more fucking attention to what anyone else is doing, mmkay? Right now. Stem the arterial spurt of your worth by keeping your eyes on your own paper from here on in.

This is non-negotiable.

The most confident people in the world don't pay an ounce of attention to what their so-called competition is up to. Because they know they have no true competition. They know they are enough as they are, and that their only job is to bring it.

Let's take a step back for a second and look at the truth of the matter. If you made a list of all of your accomplishments, no matter how small — all of your triumphs, all of the opportunities that you created for yourself, all of the times you over-delivered on something (whether it was noticed or not), all of the times you were strong and showed up when it would have been easier to hide — what would you think of that person? In fact, put this book down right now and start writing. Start downloading from your brain all of the examples you can think of. Right down to when you defended someone at school when you were 13.

Done? Then clearly you can see you're an awesome human being. Being human is really tough and if you've made it a few decades in *plus* you're working for yourself, you have *every* reason to be megatronically confident because you're doing better in the self-belief arena than about 80% of humans.

"Yeah, but Heather...there are better, more talented coaches/artists/ accountants/web designers/CEOs/agency owners/etc. than me."

So what? Why is that a reason to not feel confident? You do you. And you are really freaking good at what you do right now.

Because you care.

Because you have standards.

Because you don't over-promise and under-deliver.

Think about it for a minute: have you ever noticed someone

(especially in the online business world) doing really well but when you delve a little deeper, watching their videos or joining their newsletter to get their Super Amazing Guide to XYZ, you realize it's the same old same old, just rehashed? And that they're not even that talented or charismatic?

Yes, there are lots of really smart exceptional people running recognizable brands, but there are equally as many mediocre people who are making bank because they're in love with self-promo and saying the right things.

In fact, I would hypothesize that truly intelligent people have a hard time being as successful as middle-of-the-road folks because we overthink things.[6] Innovative multi-passionate folks hate putting anything out into the world that feels pedestrian. We don't like repeating the same message, and we get bored with what marketing requires of us.

So give yourself credit, friend! And then think about how that translates into how you show up.

It's not magic, it's mindset. And mindset is a decision.

It's deciding to give yourself credit, owning your expertise, holding your shoulders back, thinking before you speak, and not giving a shit what other people think. Yes, including that potential client on the other side of the screen! I don't need you to convince me or impress me. I need you to show me that the decision I'm almost ready to make is the right one.

---

6 There's a growing body of psychological studies showing the correlation between intelligence and overthinking, including the effects of such correlation on creativity and output. For example: https://www.ncbi.nlm.nih.gov/pmc/articles/PMC3269637/

"But I haven't...y'know...arrived yet!"

I hear that a lot. But here's the thing: you don't have to wait to be invited. There is no external change in circumstance that you need to be waiting for. No, you don't have to have a degree after your name.

You belong at the table at all stages of your evolution. It doesn't matter where you are on the spectrum of knowledge. There will always be people less knowledgeable than you. The only thing that matters is that you don't misrepresent yourself. So pull up a chair and show us what you've got.

> You have a right to be here.
> You don't need to ask permission.
> No pre-emptive apologies required.
>
> There is no entry fee or degree.
>
> You have a right to be here.
> To speak your mind. To share your art.
> To hold a difference of opinion.
>
> No need to achieve expert status first.
> You are already an expert to all the souls
> who have yet to cross the bridges you have.
>
> You have a right to be here.
> To show your work. To take a seat at the table.
> To learn from those you admire
> and to be of service to those who admire you.
>
> Build a rich relationship with your fears.

Hold them close and look them in the eye
until you see they're just little kids in the night
frightened of a non-existent boogeyman.

You have a right to be here.
With all of your uncertainties, flaws, secrets, and regrets.
This is what makes you human.
This is why your place at the table is so important.
Leave your perfection out in the cold night.

Bring in your empathy, curiosity, and gifts.
Bring in your unbridled enthusiasm to do something
worth getting excited for and come take your place 'round the fire.
You have a right to be here.

From: https://republicoffreedom.com/you-have-a-right-to-be-here/

One final note on confidence

It's super important not to equate confidence with assholery. It's easy to have that misconception because often the loudest of the confident *are* assholes or have egos that can barely fit into the coworking space.

But I'm quite certain that if you become amazingly confident you're not going to automagically turn into an asshole. Confidence is like wealth: having it doesn't change you, it amplifies what's there. In fact, it's primarily the lovely, kind, and caring among us who stress about this. So if you're not an asshole now, you probably won't be one later.

Being confident is a superpower. It is such a reward in and of itself. And there's no real downside. If you're nice and kind, you'll inspire the heck out of people because we like to see good people rise.

Confidence is rocket fuel. You get to go out into the world and make shit happen. Who wouldn't want that?

Decisiveness

Decisiveness is a critical skill to develop because from here on in, you're the one steering the ship. You're not working for someone else anymore. So you have to make decisions all the time — *literally* all the time. Little micro-decisions, big macro-decisions. They're primarily on your shoulders now. And they're going to be on your shoulders until that point (if it's part of your master plan) that you can start putting people in place under you and letting them make the decisions.

You're at the helm, and in your business-building phase being wishy-washy means missed opportunities.
Being indecisive wastes time.
Being indecisive wastes money.
Being indecisive wastes value because if you're sitting there hemming and hawing and unable to make a decision, you're shooting yourself in the foot.
You even run the risk of marring your own reputation. People don't trust people who can't shit or get off the pot.

Your entire job is to make decisions, all the time, forever. (Yay!) So it's high time to get good at it, isn't it? (By the way, ALL of Chapter 10 is about decision-making so this is just the set up to illustrate what a key skill decisiveness is.)

"But Heather, what if I fuck it up?"

That's fine. You're going to make tons of wrong decisions. Go for it. You have to do that. That's a rite of passage. Bad decisions are coming.

Fortify yourself for when you make the wrong decisions, but know that it's not a *problem*. It's part of the journey.

Make the wrong decision, see it as a data point, and keep on moving. That's why I've been preparing you to keep judgment out of it. The wrong decisions that you make aren't going to be wrong because you suck. They're going to be wrong because you didn't have enough data points to make the right decision at that time.

You can't let it knock your confidence. Chalk it up to experience and then keep on going because our need for you to show up with Your Great Work is more important than your hurt feeling from a suboptimal decision.

I'm so tired of phenomenal people with excellent ideas letting themselves get in their own way. I want to see people shine. I want to see them confident. I want to help them become who they really want to be in this life. And the only way to do that is through making decisions and improving each time.

Micro-improvements are an entrepreneur's superpower. I know we all want to hatch out of the egg just being awesome and having companies that kick ass and take names, but that ain't how it works. It's pretty much always a slow burn. But it's the slow burn of excellence. It's the slow burn of discernment. It's the slow burn of a visionary pulling together the pieces, shifting, testing, learning, scrapping, shifting, and so on and so forth until you have a business or a body of work that's truly worth owning.

How do I act if decisiveness isn't my thing?

It's fine if you're indecisive. It's not fine if you plan to do nothing about it. I'll be the first to admit that I used to be extremely indecisive.

And I mean *extreme*. I'm 10 million times better now, partially because of what I like to think of as the "immersion therapy" I went through when I took Seth Godin's altMBA program. I learned how to be decisive because I was given time pressure. I didn't have the choice of *not* making a decision.

Your lack of decisiveness is just a protective measure. Many of us don't like to live with the responsibility of our decision, even if it's small. ("If I choose Mexican takeout for the family and the burritos are bland, everyone will blame me!") The thing is, it's never as bad as your brain makes it out to be. Imagine you're afraid of snakes and someone throws you into a snake pit until you're like, "Actually, these snakes aren't so bad." That's where we're going with this.

In other words, you're going to have to bite the bullet and do some immersion therapy. That means actually making decisions, on the regular. Here's how you can do it without throwing your nervous system into a tizzy:

1. Reframe your conception of risk. Hey look, you already did that in Chapter 2! If you've forgotten what that feels like, flip back to that chapter and breeze through it again.

2. Make literally any decision.

I'm not kidding. Start with the lowest-level decision and don't duck out of chances to decide. If your partner's like, "What takeout do you want to get for dinner?" and you're like, "Meh, whatever you feel like." Yeah, quit that, Jenny. Nobody likes people who have no opinions.

Every little decision builds your decision muscle. Not sure which sweater to wear to the Everything's Better in a Sweater party? Just bite the bullet and choose. Don't overthink things.

Don't know which mailing list provider to go with? Flip a coin. (They're all similar anyway.) Get in the habit of deciding and *build. that. muscle.*

Understand that your decisions are by and large completely reversible. It's not like you're tattooing it on the face of the Internet. By practising decision-making in little (regular, reversible) baby steps, you'll gain the confidence you need as you go.

If nothing else...

Start by defining what you *don't* want. That's a decision too.

This is easy to overlook and yet *critically important*. So what do you *not* want to invite into your business? Penny-pinching clients? Independent contractors that ghost you? Shitty pens? There are a bunch of micro-decisions that go into avoiding the things you don't want in your business. Start there...it's fun. Most of us are pretty clear on what we can't stand anyway.

Perseverance

Why do we need perseverance? Because entrepreneuring is really hard. And the necessity of perseverance is very unsexy. Nobody talks about it. Perseverance doesn't sell.

You know, success doesn't happen overnight, which is a ridiculous cliché but it's true. Things take a shitload of time and you have to believe that when you put in the work and when you play the long game that things will start to come to fruition. And to play the long game, you have to have a strong sense of perseverance as a major piece of your personality. You can't be someone who's going to give up easily because the people who give up easily are the people who don't run their own business, period.

The fuel for perseverance isn't just believing in the end goal, it's a belief that what you do in the day-to-day matters. And not just that it matters, but that you like it.

If you don't like the day-to-day work that you're doing, you won't have staying power. And if you don't have staying power, you won't be able to see things through. I don't mean that you won't be able to see things through to the end, I mean you won't be able to show up consistently. If you don't find meaning in the stuff that sometimes feels like drudgery, it won't last.

Now, does this mean that you only do fun stuff? Heyyll no.

I was reading a book by Canadian astronaut Chris Hadfield recently, and he talked about how preparation to go into space was a process of years and years (and years and years) of doing things that most people don't like to do. Things like training and taking tests and learning new skills and learning Russian and studying engineering in Russian. It was really just a long series of building skills and knowledge and being tested on it with no guarantee of any payoff in the end. There was literally a very slim possibility that going into space would ever become a reality for him.

And it's fascinating because we tend to think of success as the sum of our accomplishments. But for Chris, he said what was important was that he loved engaging in the process and that he didn't judge his merit on whether or not he made it into space. He judged his merit on whether he showed up every day and put in the work so that he would be prepared if the opportunity ever presented itself.

This kind of attitude is so critical for people who operate outside of the working norms. It's so critical for creative people to think differently about how we show up. Yes, sure, we need to make a living, that was never a question. But we didn't escape the 9-to-5 just to engage in further drudgery. We escaped the 9-to-5 so that we could choose to engage in the things that light us up.

Perseverance becomes second nature because we believe so deeply that what we do matters on a day-to-day basis. And for me, it's fueled by the knowledge that going back into the Matrix would kill me.

It's either persevere and make this work...or the gulag.

It's find the answers I need to continue building a body of work that matters, that helps people...or give up on myself entirely.

Because that's what going back would mean: losing all belief in myself and my value as a creative, dynamic human that has resources at my fingertips.

Perseverance reminds you that it's important to know who you are, where you stand, and why you stand there. Because if you're a person without convictions, it's hard to continue on. It's hard to believe in yourself, and your work, and in the people who support you doing what you do.

Perseverance is *born* out of conviction. Perseverance is saying "this matters."

Perseverance is also saying "I'm pretty sure this matters," even when it feels like everything sucks and it's all going to shit.

Perseverance is saying "I'm doing this anyway," even when no one believes in you.

Perseverance is when you continue on even though it seems like the only person that it matters to in the world is you. When you know that you're reason enough.

If you're thinking something along the lines of "Fuck me, Heather, this sounds hard," you're exactly right.

We're socialized to look for formulas. We're surrounded by easy fixes and stories of (apparently) "overnight" successes. Buying into this will absolutely hamstring your perseverance though.

Setting your expectations according to that timeline will eventually make you feel like a failure.

Because as a business owner, you're always assessing your current situation against where you want to be and where you need to be, especially where you need to be financially, right? And so you're like, "OK, right now I'm running out of my savings" or "My company is paying for my life, but not much more" or "I have a little bit to roll into the business. But where I really want to be one year from now is making six-plus figures."

If you fall prey to the heavily massaged "truths" on the Internet, you will be disappointed.

And that's why you've got to harness perseverance. When you're eight months in and have barely budged your revenue? Perseverance, baby.

But what if you really, really try to persevere and are still having problems?

If you're having trouble continuing along the path that you're currently meandering down, it's probably worth looking at some of the deeper issues. Sometimes the trouble is down to the simple (and more surface-level) fact that you're not able to meet your financial needs. And a money deficit is one of the quickest ways to take the wind out of your sails.

But sometimes it's deeper than that.

Sometimes it's a lack of self-belief.

Sometimes it's the mindfuck of feeling like you are just performing another routine because you haven't "found your passion" yet. (Fuck finding your passion. Identify your *fingerprint*.)

Sometimes it's because you were chasing freedom instead of what you really wanted, which was agency.

Oh, lordy...there's never *not* some shit to unpack when you leave the Matrix.

Consistency

If someone came to me and asked, "If you could boil down the secrets behind your successes to one overarching thing, what would it be?" I'd say, "Consistency."

Consistency is everything. Ev-er-y-thing. All the other pieces I'm talking about here matter...but without consistency, it all falls apart. And I mean consistency in every way.

Consistency in how you show up.
Consistency in how you treat people.

Consistency in how you treat yourself.
Consistency in the work.
Consistency in your habits.
Consistency in your output.
Consistency in business presence.
Consistency in respecting the process.
Consistency in respecting that the hardest work is often the work worth doing.

This doesn't mean you can never take a break and you always have to be "on." It means you have to develop the habits of success and make them non-negotiable. I know I sound like Steven Covey with this "habits of success" stuff, but it's just the reality of it all. It's what makes the difference between the mediocre and the great. And I don't know about you, but I want to look back on my life and be really proud of what I built. I want it to be great!

Making consistency a habit

I'm not going to pretend like I'm some bastion of unwavering regularity. Quite the opposite, if I'm honest, because I have the attention span of a drunken louse. (That's the singular of lice, if you didn't know. Now you can impress people with your linguistic prowess at parties.)

Take me, writing this book. I'm supposed to write every day, but I just spent two weeks eating whole boxes of After Eights over the holidays, *thinking* about writing rather than actually doing it. I fell off the wagon hard. And getting back on it has been a biatch. But, it's non-negotiable. *I must ship this work.* I have to dig back in. No one is telling me to. I don't have a book deal at the time of this writing. I'm not beholden to anyone. No one is clutching their pearls waiting for the release date. But I have to fucking do it because the work matters to me and if I'm not accountable to my own dreams, then no one is going to do it for me.

The thing about consistency and work that matters is this: Work that matters is rarely urgent. But it's incredibly important. When you have important work to do (like writing a book), the resistance is going to come out of nowhere like a bag of rocks hitting you in the head again and again.

You'll find 1,001 things that need to get done before you can settle in and do the important stuff. Your mind will find all kinds of fires that need to be put out first (that's why the Pause Inbox tool is genius for creative people).

So, let's dig into this a little more so you can go out there and actually know what you're doing when it comes to consistency.

The two kinds of consistency

The way I see it, there are two kinds of consistency:
  - Consistency in the tangibles (e.g., newsletter frequency, social media, background business tasks like bookkeeping), and
  - Consistency in the way you show up.

Consistency in the tangibles is what you want to create habits around. Successful people don't just wake up and do all the things they're supposed to do better than you. They create systems that leverage their strengths and support their weaknesses. Look at Richard Branson: he's famous for having a very short attention span and therefore carries a little notebook around with him to capture ideas and when it's not handy he writes them on his hand. Otherwise, poof! Gone. He has a shorter attention span than most of us by all accounts, but the dude bought himself an island by the time he was 28 so you can't tell me he hasn't created some habits for consistency.

Here's what I do: I make some things in my business non-negotiable.

And then I schedule them into my calendar. Simple as that. And the thing is, if I *don't* follow through, I'm disrespecting someone else's time down the line from me. It may be a client who's waiting for feedback, or a reader who's expecting my weekly newsletter. If I have systems in place so that people know what to expect from me, I have to be accountable otherwise I damage my own credibility.

OK, so what about consistency in *the way* you show up? That's where it's really critical that you do you, and you do it well. If you have an image that you're trying to keep up, it's going to get really exhausting and smart people will eventually see through it. I've known relationship coaches who were a hot mess behind the scenes with their primary partner and eventually their image imploded.

And then there's the proliferation of "business gurus" who brag about six-figure launches but fail to mention that they spent 80% of that launch revenue on Facebook ads and a launch manager, and have precious little *actual* profit leftover in the end. Was it really worth all the stress and the $75,000 spent on Facebook ads for your $7,000 profit, Sandra? I don't mean to disparage people who do this. It takes a lot of courage and a lot of work to pull that kind of thing off. But the thing is, people will eventually see through this because it's not sustainable.

When you see something that's too good to be true, you've gotta ask yourself, "Where is the lie?"

Consistency in the way you show up is all about integrity. It's about being in integrity with your values, and operating with integrity in business. You know what I think are the two most wonderful compliments one can get as a business owner in this Internet age where images are pretty easy to manufacture?

"He/she's the real deal."

and

"You're exactly the same in real life as I experience you online."

Boom! That *means* something! That is currency right there. It means you've been consistent in the way you show up. It means you've been operating with integrity. It means you haven't been fooling anyone.

The thing about consistency in the way you show up is that it earns you something very, very precious, and that's what my friend smarty-pants Illana Burk calls "authority capital." Authority capital is the reason I can now get away with being a little less consistent with things like regular newsletters. I've earned enough authority capital by being consistent that people know who I am now after nine years in business. And to a degree, my reputation precedes me. That is such a huge gift in so many ways, but it was a gift that was earned. It wasn't by accident, and it sure as shit wasn't manifested. I put in the time to earn people's trust and now they have my back. And I swear on my movie-dad Robin Williams's grave that I will never take that trust for granted.

In fact, when you have a degree of authority capital, you get the privilege of bringing people along the next part of the journey with you. They are already IN. They want to see what's next: What do you have to teach? What do you have to show?

It's a really exciting place to be and anyone can get there, but it's all down to consistency.

The secret to consistency (that you've already totally figured out)

One final thing you need to understand about consistency is that it's rooted in the why (or unique fingerprint) of your work. Being grounded in that bigger picture stuff, and calling on your anchor as I spoke about in Chapter 6, is how you keep coming back to the work when you get tired and feel like you don't want to do the consistent things anymore.

This is such an important thing for you to understand *first*, and ground your business in, because otherwise you'd just be doing it for money. And believe me, not only does that kind of motivation not stand the test of time, but it'll also burn you out.

There are people who are consistently showing up but they're unsuccessful at the growth element. They're unsuccessful at the longevity. They're unsuccessful at being able to see the bigger picture and strategize towards it. And it's probably because their business idea is rooted in something that was just meant to actually pay the bills as opposed to the deeper work that they are called to do.

Let's take the example of someone who starts as a web designer. And then they get to the stage where they can't move past the glass earnings ceiling that they've made for themselves. Then they're like, "In the process of being a web designer, I've learned so much about branding, so I reinvented myself as a branding expert." And then they start doing branding for the same $$ they were charging for websites, getting by on that but not able to grow their business meaningfully beyond a dollars-for-hours model. And after a while that gets boring and then they're like, "Oh, now I'm a tarot card reader."

Umm, who are you? What is it that you're actually trying to do here, because it sounds like you are literally jumping from job to job and continuing to hit your head on that ceiling.

If you don't have a deep self-awareness and you're not more rooted in the bigger picture of what you're trying to do in the world, then that glass ceiling is never going to go away. You'll continue to pursue other short-term skill-based fixes, but they'll fizzle.

There's a difference between people who jump from thing to thing and those who do very disparate things like own a business consulting company plus a polar expedition company and have it make perfect business sense. With the latter, there's a through-line in that the businesses and its founder are mission-driven instead of just trying to make ends meet. Because if you're a web designer and a VA, let's be honest, Zarah, you're trying to make ends meet.

Let me be clear: *This is not meant as a judgment call. It's a gentle warning to go into things eyes wide open.* Figuring out that underlying mission should be part of the legwork of your first business iterations. It's why I made you sit through so much internal stuff before we ever even got to things like cognitive load and system gaming. So if you happened to skip through that stuff to get to the "real business" stuff, then pause and go back, because that? That's what's going to make or break your business. Truly.

Curiosity

This probably seems a bit trite because it's one of those Steve Jobs–isms we see all over the place. But staying curious doesn't come naturally to a lot of creative minds. We might be curious about how to do something creative, but staying curious about the things that aren't easy for us, or that don't seem interesting on first glance, is much harder. In other words, creative entrepreneurs need to stay curious about their end user. There is no set-it-and-forget-it business model that's sustainable over time. We need to look at the data, even if the data freaks us out.

I believe the most important reason why you need curiosity is that otherwise it's very quick and easy to fall into tunnel vision. It's very easy to think that you've already figured something out, or that you know the best way, or that someone else did it that way so you're sticking to it.

To be honest, tunnel vision is the death knell to any enterprise. Even to self-employment. A lot of clients of mine show up with a certain degree of tunnel vision in the beginning and that's what I have to yank them out of.

You have to stay curious, and you have to be open. You have to be constantly reassessing things, and that's very uncomfortable for people. They want to make choices (that are the "right" choices) and be done with it.

And fine, you can try to do that. And you can probably get by. But if you want to really be in the game, and see opportunities, you've got to be perpetually inquisitive.

Staying curious about the people we serve (and seek to serve) with our work is the best way to ensure that our business will be sustainable over time. In fact, I would go so far as to say that staying curious is what will help you best build a legacy with your work. Because in the end, it's not about what you have to give as much as how what you have to give helps and serves others.

I've worked with so many business owners who were just slightly out of alignment on this one aspect. They were too focused on what they were trying to share/teach/create rather than what their end user truly needed. And when they shifted that one aspect, everything changed.

Staying curious, listening, allowing yourself the space to hear what your people need, paying attention to what went wrong when things went wrong, paying attention to what went right when things went right...it all matters. You need to be a detective. You need to be the visionary that knows the nuances of your business and your end users better than anyone.

Do what you need to do. Poll your mailing list. Send personal emails to your most loyal followers, even if you only have five. Our audience is never too small to do this, and it's never too late to start either.

But Heather, I'm not curious/I'm too busy to be curious/curiosity is a luxury!

Oh for Pete's sake, yes you are curious. It's a human thing. I can tell you that in the immediate moment if you're feeling very uncurious about your business it could be because your cognitive load is too heavy. (Remember that whole thing in Chapter 6? Yeah, it's never going away. Refer back to it anytime you feel like you're too burnt out to be curious.)

Curiosity is a choice. It's the choice to be continually present. It's easy to not care because you're just straight-up busy, and feel like you don't have the bandwidth to think abstractly about your business. But that doesn't mean it doesn't matter.

Let me phrase this differently: Being serious about understanding humans in your business is a professional choice. It's a differentiator. This isn't as simple as wrapping your brain around Google Analytics. It's the nuances of paying attention to the evolving needs of your customers, your team, and various other stakeholders. It's listening to what's underneath what's being said. And it should supersede your "busyness."

In fact, it's extra important to be curious when you're busy and when you think you don't have time for it because that's when things can go sideways.

Generosity

I'm going to start with saying this:

Generosity is not the same as people-pleasing.
Generosity is not the same as self-sacrifice.
You do not need to remove something from your plate in order to fill up someone else's.

Generosity in the entrepreneurial world is about giving people chances to show up fully and it's about making sure that the right people get the credit they deserve. We've all been on the wrong end of someone else either taking or getting credit for work we've put our heart into. This is extremely ungenerous of the perpetrators. Don't be that person. It's a dick move.

Generosity is also about taking the time to advocate for people who may not be in a position to advocate for themselves. Again, we've all been in a position at some point in time where someone who had a lot more sway than us went to bat for us and it meant the world.

Generosity also means paying people their worth. I'm going to bet that if you're a small business owner reading this book, then you work occasionally with freelancers or independent contractors. Sure, it's easy to play the "I don't have enough money for that" card when you're growing a business and funds are limited. But then it's your job to find a freelancer who you *can* afford for the services you need. Haggling on price is a jerk move and it devalues the work of all independent workers.

Great leadership is generous. We happily follow leaders that build us up and believe in our capacity...that show us where the opportunity is and then encourage us to step into that space. Management and leadership should be closely aligned, but alas, this isn't so common in real life. All too many of us have had experiences of working under managers who have little-to-no leadership skills at all. You know... those managers who are unapproachable and punitive.

And come on...there's nothing more dehumanizing in the workplace than a manager who treats you like you're incompetent and makes themselves very difficult to communicate with. These people shouldn't be managers. You either 'get' leadership and are open to learning how to be a good leader, or...you don't get the privilege of that position. (At least that's how it is in my imaginary universe!)

The leader of a team I was once on asked me in private why his "leadership strategy" seemed to be backfiring, and why everyone was so grumpy. I told him it was partially because every time we had a team meeting he took a big shit on everyone first, telling them what they were doing wrong and that they had to do better, only sometimes ending on a complimentary note. (For reference, this was a highly competent and seasoned team.) When I told him he should try leading with generosity, recognizing great work and empowering the team to do better in the areas we weren't tight enough, his response was, "I don't subscribe to that." Unsurprisingly, he continued to be an asshole and has never gained the respect he so desperately wanted.

The funny thing is that if you're the leader, whether on a team or the leader of a company, you've already made it to the top! You have no reason *not* to be generous and help empower those under you to bring the best of themselves.

All this to say that as an entrepreneur, you're likely in a leadership position whether you like it or not. You've created something new. You set the tone of that entity. Even if you're a company of one, you're still a leader. And great leadership is generous.

It all comes down to this

I believe generosity is one of the most powerful things you can inject into the ethos of your business. It is life changing. It is business altering.

All it takes are the simple acts of being a generous person, a generous manager, a generous boss, treating people like human beings, giving them leeway, trusting them to make great decisions, trusting them to step into their own, paying people fair wages, etc. OK...so it's perhaps not so simple, as this requires us to design generous systems in our business from the get-go. But it's worth it!

It's bringing the humans back into business. I don't understand why this is such a weird concept for so many. It's not a nice-to-have. It's a *necessity* in this day and age if you want to stand out. If you want to be exceptional.

And the reality is that because consumers want to feel respected, generosity has become a financial driver. You want to make bank? You want to be super successful? Crank up your fricken' generosity. Forget about your growth hacks. Those are very 2009.

If you bake generosity into your business, you'll be laughing all the way to the bank. You've still gotta persevere and you've still gotta play the long game. But insert generosity as part of the mission and culture. People want that. They miss that because *it's not common.* There's that old adage that people forget what you did but they remember how you made them feel. Nothing could be truer than true.

Bonus? This is one of the key things that'll keep you going when the going gets tough. It helps you get over yourself; by focusing on other people, you can't get too caught up in your own neuroses.

PART 3
WHAT YOU NEED TO DO

Strategy vs. Tactics

HOLY CATS — YOU MADE IT to the final third of the book! Nice work. When you first picked up this tome, you probably weren't expecting it to be quite like this, because this isn't how business books are normally written. Business books normally just tell you how to *do* business things, whereas this book is teaching you how to *be* the business owner you want to be.

We have covered a ton of material on everything from the unique fingerprint of your business right through to how you make sure you actually do what you say you're going to do on a regular basis. That's a lot of thinking! It's a lot of deep work and you've got to give yourself a pat on the back for not shying away from it.

Everything that we've talked about is the internal work. It's the preparation for execution.

And here's the thing: as I've said before, entrepreneurship is never a one-and-done. In the most simplistic sense you've got to think, then you've got to act, then you've got to think, and then you've got to act. It is literally a constant evolution. So of course, now that you've waded through the cerebral stuff, you need to start thinking about what the practical steps are. What's the next phase now that you've really rooted yourself in who you are as a business owner and you know what kind of internal skills you need to then execute on these next steps?

Most entrepreneurs and wannabe entrepreneurs never get this level of understanding about themselves, or they stumble into it after years. But you've done that intentionally and now you have the grounding to use it properly, so massive kudos to you, friend.

Having done all this work, you'll now be able to learn all the tactical stuff on a deeper level *and* actually use it in a way that works for you. That is the nature of entrepreneurship. We act. That's what we do.

You.
Are.
Ready.

Woop! Champagne and chanterelles all around, in proper Swedish style.

Strategy and tactics

Buckle up because we're going to dive straight into strategy and tactics. Why? Because the world doesn't need any more spray marketing.[7]

If you don't have a good grasp on this already, then it's important to understand the difference between the use of strategy and tactics, and

---

7 Spray marketing is when you have no direction but just do a bunch of random shit to get in front of as many people as possible because the Internet said so.

how the employment of thought-through strategy and tactics is more effective than just *taking random action*.

If you don't have a strategy behind whatever it is you're doing, you'll just be doing things for the sake of doing them. Even worse, you'll be running a business that's inherently reactive instead of the much more manageable (and mental health–friendly) proactive. Truth be told, there's really no point in having a strategy without tactics, or tactics without a strategy.

So, how do we define these?

A *strategy* is the bigger-picture roadmap that lays out the path for you to move towards a goal or a set of goals for your business.

Tactics are the individual actions you take that support the strategy or the roadmap to your goals.

Let's look at some examples:

A *strategy* would be to grow your mailing list with qualified leads. A tactic would be to run a 30-day challenge to achieve that.

A *strategy* would be to increase customer loyalty with the aim of creating repeat customers. A *tactic* would be to send everyone who purchases your service/product a reusable bag with your logo and a badass slogan on it.

I know for some this will be an oversimplification, while for others this might be an aha moment. Whenever you're looking at your plans for the coming quarter, just make sure you are clear on the strategy you're implementing (and why) and, secondarily, the tactics you'll implement to serve that strategy.

The key is that your strategy must be grounded in your foundational "this is who I am" piece. If you're not clear on your unique fingerprint, you'll be tempted to create strategies based on someone else's ideas of success for your business. When you know who you are, you're better equipped to notice the quick fixes and recognize those "sounds nice, but no thank you" moments. It allows you to dodge bullets and keep iterating towards the thing that actually feels the most resonant for you.

A really great example is the story I recently read about Jenn Harper of Cheekbone Beauty. Jenn is a Canadian indigenous woman and entrepreneur who started a makeup company because she saw the need for "...a brand for real people, that not only offered makeup that influenced trends but that was also not intimidating for those who are new to the world of makeup. There needed to be a brand that was made in Canada, that's never tested on animals *and* that gave back to the First Nations community."[8] She was on *Dragons' Den* and got offered a huge amount of investment capital from some dude who wanted 50% ownership of her business and she was like, "Nah, I'm not feelin' you." (I'm paraphrasing, but that was the gist.)

I mean she'd been trying in earnest to get someone to invest in her business for ages and then this guy comes along with wads of cash to invest and she's like, "Mmm. No."

Why? Because Jenn knows who she is and she knows what she's trying to do with that brand, so she's not going to fall for the short-term fix. Moving in that direction strategically would completely undermine everything about what she wants for her business.

So to recap, knowing who you are and what you stand for in your

8 https://cheekbonebeauty.ca/pages/meet-the-founder

204   HEATHER THORKELSON

business is your entrepreneurial life preserver. Hold onto that like your life depends on it, and develop your growth strategies without letting go.

What a solid strategy will do for you

Save you from shiny object syndrome

Having a solid strategy is gonna save your ass from so, so many things. Let's start with the most obvious one, shiny object syndrome. Maybe not all of it, but most of it. I know you have a bunch of PDFs and courses you've paid for that are languishing on your hard drive or that you've forgotten the login for after completing the first module. We all do!

Of course we fall for this stuff because we just desperately want someone to show us how.

But as you probably know (because you're reading this book), it's mostly smoke and mirrors. They're selling you shortcuts that either don't work or aren't sustainable. They're selling you a "product" (My Six-Month Strategy!) that took them five years to develop.

There are no shortcuts.

And quite frankly, I don't want any shortcuts.

Case in point, I was part of a huge female entrepreneur group in the early days of my business and they were all jumping on the latest tactic to massively grow their list or what have you and it just never sat right with me. I was always over in the proverbial corner with my unpopular opinion, "I'm in this for the long game. Quick hits are not how I want to do business."

And nine years later, do you know how many of those folks from the entrepreneurial group are still running their own businesses? Very, very few. If I had to take a guess based on what I can see on social media, I'd say a 15% success rate is a generous estimate.

Short-term tactics are for the starry-eyed heroines on a stage of their own dreams. And let me say that this is not a judgment. I *get* why people fall for the fantasy. I also get why the fantasy fades away and returning to a job becomes necessary. Because these people bought the story without understanding who they would need to become in order to achieve the thing they wanted so dearly. It's not fucking easy. And for most people, it doesn't come naturally.

But you...you've put in the work to avoid the lure of the quick fix. You've become a discerning customer. We need more of you. We need more people who are self-aware enough that they can make swifter and smarter "Is this right for my business?" decisions, and then carry on without missing a beat.

Help you avoid comparisonitis

You know that feeling of wanting so bad to be a part of something but you feel that you're, at best, an imposter? You desperately want to be a good speaker, blogger, parent, coach, employee, neighbour, student, leader, member of the human race, but your monkey mind tells you you're just not up to snuff? Like that feeling of being in a room full of people who seem to "get" it but you've somehow missed the plot?

That was me for about a third of my life. And I'm not exaggerating. I used to constantly, actively, and detrimentally compare myself to others on every level. It was like a hobby. It was a shitty hobby that left me feeling like I was never enough. I would compare myself to others on the way I looked, the way I spoke, the way I reacted to things. I would even compare myself daily to the bubbly confidence of a teenage fast food cashier and wonder how the hell she could be so happy and sure of herself in front of strangers. (Dumb comparison, considering I'm an introvert.) Literally everywhere I looked there were people who were excelling at the everyday things that I found cripplingly difficult.

I would also compare things that (a) were out of my control and (b) I didn't have all the information on. Like my family vs. my friends' families. I would wonder what it was like to be a part of a loving, accepting family unit that got along so great and then feel like shit because I didn't have that. I told myself I was at a huge disadvantage because of it.

I craved it.
I felt jealous.
I didn't understand why I got the short end of the stick.

And while it occurred to me logically that other people's families probably weren't perfect, it was easier to ignore that and live in the comfort of me vs. them. Because life is easier when you break it down into black and white.

Except for when it's not.

Seeing things in black and white, me vs. them, eventually got really old. It started to piss me off because frankly, I'm smarter than that. It was a coping mechanism. Something to fall back on. An excuse not to do the work I needed to do to get to a better, more confident, more fully expressed headspace.

My thoughts started to make me mad. I heard the victim inside my head and I wanted to shake her hard and say, "You know better than this. You *are* better than this. Stop using comparison as a crutch!"

Then a shift began in my mid-20's. I was super-fucking-over playing small and shrinking from what should (and could) be the building of an incredible life. I was done battling with my self-esteem and was ready to let my self-worth enter the ring and duke it out for the win.

That's when the real work started. That's when I began forcing my courage to show up every time it wanted to hide. That's when I began looking at why I was allowing myself to benchmark my life and talents against everyone else's.

And 15 years later I'm a completely different person.

Not that it took me an entire 15 years to change, and not to say that there weren't setbacks! Comparisonitis still tries to poke his craptastic little head around the corner when I branch into new areas in life. When I started studying at university, when I started working after university, when I left the corporate world and didn't know what in heck I was going to do with my life...

Although *everyone compares*, and we often compare around the same topics ("I wish I had her legs"), no two comparisons are alike. You are a unique combination of cells, upbringing, and experience that exists only once in the universe, and so only you experience negative thoughts the way you do, for the precise reasons you do.

Just like any emotional response, there are usually specific precursors that set off this self-defeating thought process. And just like certain songs will make you (and only you) teary-eyed, certain circumstances are the early warning system that your monkey mind might decide to take you for a run through the shit swamp.

So here's where I'm going to call you out on any comparisonitis you might be suffering from right this minute: you're not behind, and none of the stuff you are doing right now is a bag of crap. How do I know this? Because...

We're all doing the best we can with the tools that we have at any given time.

Stop for a second. Say that out loud. Say it until you believe it. Say it until you start feeling like you are enough.

When I say tools, I mean everything — physical, emotional, spiritual. You're guided by all of those every day. You are guided by the height of that knowledge in you at this present time, and you are a work in progress.

So. You're doing the best that you can, with the tools that you have right now. Period.

Next month you will have more tools, more knowledge, more practice, more support. And next month you'll continue to do the best that you can with the tools that you have at that time. No matter how accomplished, famous, wealthy, or seemingly happy a person is, that statement is our common denominator.

It's time to rock what you've got.

And how do you do that and not get caught up in all the comparisonitis? Strategy, baby. If you've already decided what you're going to do, and not do, then that's it. You don't have to compare in the moment, or get jealous whenever you see something new come on the scene. Because your mission, and the way you're going to live and work it, aren't up for grabs anymore. Which means you can keep your eyes on your own page, and ignore everyone else.

Free you from perfection

Perhaps one of the absolute best benefits of mission-based strategy is that it gives you license to be as imperfect as you need to be in order to iterate meaningfully. In other words, if the mission is right and resonant, then you can fail in your iterations as many times as you like.

You are free to experiment. Your tactics are no longer *do or die* because you know that whatever happens, you're doing it in service of a solid strategy based on your mission and thus the outcomes are *just information.*

Case in point, I like to refer to this book you're reading right here as my *shitty first book*. I don't actually think it's shitty, but I've never written a book before so I know it's not going to be my absolute best work. I'm learning how to write a book as I type this! I know I'm a good writer, so that's a start. But writing a whole gahddamb book is another story entirely.

If I let perfection get in the way of good enough, I'd never ship this work.

And the truth is that I already know that 20 years and a few books later I'll likely look back on this and think, "Hmmm, my first book was pretty good, but look how far I've come as an author." I'll be thinking about how much the way I express myself has changed, but that it had a lot of value at the time. It served its purpose and it still holds value... it's just that it was my 'shitty first book'.

I'm not promising this book will be *perfect*, which right there allows for imperfection. I'm also not afraid of judgment. I know it's coming. I know some people will think this book is a bag of crap. And that's OK — I am not for everyone. If someone I respect and admire thinks it's shitty, I'll definitely feel the pangs of that. But pangs aren't going to kill or dismember me. And it won't discourage me from learning to do better next time. Because I'm not here to be perfect. I'm here to be of service.

I'm also not doing this book-writing thing alone. Remember how I said I've never done this before and I don't know what I'm doing? So, obviously, I've asked for help. I have a developmental editor who is guiding me through the process and a handful of smart folks who are at the ready to proofread my final draft. If I sound like an idiot or if my concepts don't make sense, they'll catch it. They're familiar with my mission and get where I'm going strategically, so having people beyond myself involved in the birth of my work helps further free me from perfection.

To recap: This book won't be perfect when it's done. But it will be good enough. And it will be extremely useful to some. Perhaps even many! Most importantly, my ideas will be out of my head and into the world where they will get the chance to help others.

That's something to get excited about. So no matter what your work, no matter what it is that you ship, let's get some shitty first drafts out there.

Components of a good strategy

Now we're going to break this down a little more into tangible components so you know what you need to incorporate into your strategy. (I promised I was going to get into specifics, didn't I?)

While it's necessary to be grounded in your mission, you also need to have the following.

A clear goal or endpoint

I mean, duh. Yet strangely enough, there are loads of business owners out there that don't have a clear goal for their current strategic plan. Or, they have a goal in the beginning, but then that goal becomes a moving target when their strategy doesn't pan out as expected. We need to get a grip on this process. Goals should be clear, measurable, and achievable based on where you're standing right now. Even if it's a stretch goal.

An understanding of the resources you currently have

Back when I started my business in 2011 I made a video series for my website opt-in and one of the videos talked about exactly this: understanding the resources you have access to right now. People, connections, free services, sources of funding that can help you... you name it! One of the first things I do when I start working with clients 1:1 is delve into the untapped resource pool that is their existing network. It's amazing what you can find hiding in plain sight.

An understanding of your stakeholders

This includes the people in your immediate life, your customers, your customers' customers, the employees or contractors you work with, etc. There are so many people that feel the ripples of the work that you do. And while we spend a lot of time thinking about the person who pays for our goods or services, we need to think about other key stakeholders in equal measure. Who in your household is supporting your entrepreneurial work? What kind of physical and/or emotional labour are they engaged in to help you succeed? What about the people you work with laterally? A good strategy takes all of these people into account.

Think back to my example in Chapter 3 of Bob's Red Mill, and how they created a profit-sharing business model that took all key players in their business into account in order to not only make it more bulletproof but also to allow the business to be a living expression of their values.

Remember, entrepreneurship is just the medium. We're world-changing here. This is yet another reason why it's so important to be clear on your mission, because if you're not, then it's really hard to communicate that to your stakeholders and get them on board.

An understanding of your business peer group and the legacy you're a part of

Your business doesn't operate in a vacuum. You've got businesses around you both competing with and complementing your work, so any good strategy needs to have an understanding of how that affects you. With your personal peer group, you know that saying about how we are a compound of the five people we spend the most time with? Same thing goes for businesses, for better or worse. We'll talk more in-depth about understanding your spot in the constellation of businesses surrounding you and developing your business peer group in a bit, but for now, just keep this on your radar.

Take me as an example

If you're like me, you lose the plot a bit when things are too theoretical. So let's look into the brass tacks of how strategies and tactics work IRL. I'm going to give you an example of my strategy and tactics to grow my business and share my work.

Remember, back in Chapter 5 I shared that the unique fingerprint of my work in the world is to have meaningful interactions that move people forward. Externally, that translates to creating transformative experiences.

Part of my strategy to achieve this is that I'm writing a book (yes, this one) to help people become the person they need to be in order to ship their great work. I'm also developing a corresponding community to support said entrepreneurs.

To do that well I need more visibility for my work. I need to get in front of the *right people*.

To be more specific, I need to signal to the people who need what I'm dishing out.

Tactics-wise, I started by doing a big tour to Hong Kong, Norway, and Iceland in early autumn 2019 to deliver workshops to small business owners and connect with people *in person* around my ideas.

This was invaluable as there is something qualitatively different around sharing ideas with people face-to-face. What I'm saying lands differently than if read on a screen, and I get incredible insight and feedback in the moment from the exact people I have set out to serve. I mean, if your aim is meaningful interactions that help move people forward, starting in person is the obvious choice.

However, in-person isn't scalable, and I want to be able to help people everywhere, no matter their location on the globe. So in January, I led a community project — a virtual sharing of experiences from people who have some deep-ass[9] wisdom to share around owning your shit in business.

---

9 This could be taken differently from how I intend it to, but I'm leaving it in anyway!

The aim of a community project is to expand the reach and get people engaged in conversation around something that a lot of people struggle with, and that I really enjoy helping people with!

The third tactic is consistently sharing snippets of my ideas (many of which are contained in this book) via social media and generating conversation around those ideas. If you've been following me on Instagram for any length of time, you'll know what I mean.

By implementing the tactics outlined above for a good chunk of time prior to launching the book or opening a community, I'll achieve the kind of awareness for my work that's needed to get a toehold when I have an actual experience or product ready to deliver.

OK, so now that you've had a little refresher on strategy (and we're all on the same page as to what a good one looks like) and a run-through of tactics, it's time to dive into some of traps you might encounter along your journey — and, with your newly refocused strategic lens, you'll be able to navigate them in all new ways.

Cognitive Traps

WE CAN TALK BIG MISSION or strategies and tactics until we're blue in the face, but none of it is going to matter one hot bit unless you pay attention to the one thing that will KILL ALL OF YOUR DREAMS.

Am I being dramatic? Sure.
Is it needed? Yes. 100%.

This isn't even exclusive to entrepreneurship or creative work for that matter. If you're unaware, or unwilling to do the work, it will fuck up all kinds of things in your life.

Friend, we're talking *cognitive traps*. They are — quite simply — the number one way you'll undermine your work and your ideas.

Cognitive traps *trap ideas*. They make the process of moving forward so much harder than it needs to be. I like to think of them as booby traps along the path towards what you want.

Imagine: You're all fired up about your thing, walking that path like a boss, waving at the bunnies, pointing and winking at the squirrels gazing down at you from the canopy, when BLAM!! Suddenly you see someone else doing what you do, but 10 times better. Wind: exit sails stage left. #fuck

This is a classic case of the old cognitive (booby) trap of comparisonitis. We're going to cover a few here, but this is one that everyone gets.

You might be thinking, "Wait...holdupbackup...what the heck is a cognitive trap exactly?"

It's when the way you *think* about something prevents you from meaningful progress.

Aww yeah, brah...you know what I mean. You *know* your thoughts hold you back sometimes. (Often?) This paralysis often disguises itself as lack of confidence, but this chapter is going to dig deeper and name the detailed negative thought processes behind the mask that we need to be aware of as people wanting to ship great work.

Sunk costs

Let's start with my good old friend sunk costs. This is one of the most common misconceptions I see, especially in early-stage entrepreneurs. This is how David McRaney of *You Are Not So Smart* describes sunk costs[10]:

"The Misconception: *You make rational decisions based on the future value of objects, investments, and experiences.*

10 https://youarenotsosmart.com/2011/03/25/the-sunk-cost-fallacy/

The Truth: *Your decisions are tainted by the emotional investments you accumulate, and the more you invest in something the harder it becomes to abandon it."*

Sunk costs throw small business owners off all the time. And as much as we feel passionate about what we do, and never want to accept that maybe an investment we made bombed or needs to be chucked in the bin, it's extremely valuable to be able to look at a situation dispassionately so we can recognize sunk costs and let them go.

Let's say you invested $10,000 into an app, and then another company (with a much bigger development and marketing budget) launched an app that did exactly what yours does, but way better and with more features. There may be no good reason to continue on trying to bring yours to market as you'll just be throwing money away at that point while your doppelganger takes up all the market share.

Or you poured thousands into a photoshoot and rebrand with a corresponding fancy website, only to have a massive entrepreneurial identity crisis and realize that this is not how you want to show up. That the inside is no longer congruent with the outside. I'm using this example because this has happened to people I know. And then they're like, "Fuck, I spent all this money and now I just want to burn it to the ground." Or in my case, "Fuck, I'm 40,000 euro committed to this ship that I'm having to walk away from. That sucks."

Good. Go ahead: walk away or burn it down. These are sunk costs and there's no point getting hung up on them.

You're emotionally attached to the investment of both time and money that it took to get you here, but *here* is no longer going to serve the direction you're going. And that, right there, is a great way to gauge whether you should drop something like it's hot: Will this thing I feel emotionally beholden to help me/my business move forward? Or will I just be throwing good money after bad?

Whenever you find yourself obsessing over thoughts such as, "But I've come this far" or "I've spent all this money" or "I didn't get to this point just to throw in the towel on this project," check yourself. It's time to reconnect to the bigger vision and ask yourself if clinging to this project or path is pulling you away from reaching your goal. Is it dragging your energy sideways from the things that really matter?

If you're not sure, ask a trusted business brain. No, not your sister or a friend who has a side hustle that makes them $250 extra a month. Ask someone who understands sunk costs and has navigated similar challenges in business. An outside perspective is sometimes all you need to suddenly release attachment to whatever sunk costs you're grappling with.

You also need to check in with your perception of risk around sunk costs. We tend to associate risk with loss, and when we're facing the need to let go of sunk costs, it feels like a big loss. It feels like we took a gamble and failed. That we suck. But that's generally not the case at all.

You aren't taking a risk when you make a decision that at the time, with all of the data that you have, seems like the correct one. You were making the best decision possible — no one makes a stupid decision on purpose! I know it feels like a bag of dicks to let go of the effort or money invested, but to hold on to the idea that you should keep forging ahead because of prior investment is not sound.

No, it doesn't feel good. But it's the smart thing to do.

The final piece to this cognitive trap is that we don't like to live with the responsibility of the decision to abandon an idea or project. We don't want to admit failure. We don't want to answer people at parties when they say, "Didn't you invest $10k in that app?"

But you must. You must! As a smart, forward-thinking entrepreneur it's your job to make rational decisions based on the future value of objects, investments, and experiences, not hold on to the emotional investments you've accumulated prior to this moment.

Scarcity

The Misconception: *Business is like pie. There's only so much to go around and if you don't get your piece, someone else will take it. Narrowing down is the death knell to you "making it."*

The Truth: *There is no pie when it comes to service-based businesses. And narrowing down your messaging is the smartest thing you can do to stand out and build a loyal following.*

In early-stage entrepreneurship, we often say, "I need whatever money I can get. I will take whatever client I can get. I don't give a shit. I serve everybody." Instead of being thoughtful and choosing a niche and getting really clear on your client's internal dialogue you're just like, "No no, I help all women over the age of 30." What we tell ourselves is that that's from a place of wanting to help. "I'm just a helper, what can I say!"

But where it's really coming from is a place of scarcity. Meaning: "My belief is that if I narrow down I will not be able to reach enough people in order to make a living, in order to actually pull this off."

When you come from a place of scarcity you spread yourself too thin. You say yes to the wrong people and the wrong projects. And, inevitably, you end up doing more harm than good.

The flip side of this that I see in more experienced entrepreneurs is that feeling of "never enough." In the beginning, maybe replacing your corporate income was your only goal. And once you've done it, you find you're not satisfied because you're looking outwards to what other people in similar lines of work have achieved in comparison to you and suddenly feeling the pinch of not-enoughness.

To combat the scarcity trap, you need to be grounded in your mission and your version of success.

How do you uncover what success means to you? A great way is to focus on financial comfort first and get to predictable profit. Then look at how you want to feel when you do what you do.

Existing costs money. This is an inalienable fact. Therefore success, for most people, has to start from a place of financial comfort. Not wealth, not riches, not Johnny Rose-level buy-a-town (*Schitt's Creek*) money. Just financial comfort. So let's start with that as a baseline: you are comfortable and you have predictable revenue in your business and *you don't worry.*

So once you've reached that baseline, what does success look like for you beyond that? How do you want to feel in your business? How do you want other people to feel when they interact with your business? What kind of legacy are you building?

Thus, in a nutshell, the questions of success for most people are first, "How do I get to a place of financial comfort?" and second, "How do I feel really fucking good about what I do in the world?"

Comparisonitis

The Misconception: *You have to arrive at a certain place in your business* *and look the part (i.e., like someone else you've identified as having it all together) in order to be considered legit.*

The Truth: *Neither you nor your business need to look or be a certain way to be of value. There's no point at which you have "arrived" and the sky will open to rain clients upon thee.*

Fun fact! The companion trap to scarcity is comparisonitis. As I shared in the last chapter, this is a massive issue that I've struggled with myself. I know how easy it is to compare yourself to others and feel like you don't measure up.

But I'm here to confirm, re-confirm, and re-re-confirm that you don't have to *look* or *be* a certain way to be of value.

It helps, because we judge people, but it's absolutely not a precursor.

And for fuck's sake, stop looking at other people who are doing similar or adjacent things. If I had a neon sign that I could hang on all my client's foreheads, it would read, "Eyes on your own paper."

It's the only thing that matters.

If you think about anyone who's really impactful with their ideas like Paul Jarvis, Sonia Simone, Seth Godin, Joanna Wiebe, David Cain, Derek Sivers, Bernadette Jiwa...their websites either have little or no imagery of them and the structure is quite basic. Their sites are mostly just words. The ideas speak for themselves.

You can easily argue that your ideas don't matter to anyone. But let's take the example of my ideas. My ideas didn't matter in 2011. Or rather, *no one knew who I was* so my ideas didn't have the chance to matter...yet. Then I blogged weekly for about six years and though I still had less than 1,000 readers, my ideas went from not mattering to anyone but me, to mattering a little to a few people, and then to mattering quite a bit to a larger handful of people. And now, a decade later, you're reading my book.

Sure, it took some time, but I didn't get from "My ideas don't matter" to "Here you are reading my book" by comparing myself to others. No, sir.

At the beginning of my entrepreneurial journey, I started out following everybody because I wanted to learn from other people. I sincerely wanted to learn everything I needed to know in order to make this thing work, because for me there was no plan B.

I needed to become the entrepreneur that I needed to be.

I was the one that I'd been waiting for.

So I started by looking at what everyone else was doing and then deciding, "I don't want to do that" or "I don't have enough money to do that."

Yes, I looked at what everyone else was doing, *but I did it with a discerning eye* because I've always been one of those salty-ass people who's like, "Oh, everyone's wearing Vuarnet? I'm not going to wear Vuarnet."

My natural saltiness kept me from following the crowd whole hog, but I still wanted to learn what worked well and which business-building practices had integrity. But after a while I started realizing I wasn't seeing anything new, but rather the same shit rehashed over and over again. The same strategies, the same tactics, the same BS being peddled. I was still signing up for people's newsletters thinking that their PDF download might just hold the key to revolutionizing my mailing list.

And it never did. It *never did*.

And then I started *not* following everyone. I started actively unfollowing people. I got off of almost all mailing lists that I was on and I completely focused on my own shit and I was like, "OK from now on, my bar is so high that for you to get into my headspace or my social media space is going to be really fucking Fort Knox hard."

There are a lot of people I unfollowed that I actually really liked. I think they're smart and interesting, and I like their writing, but *they weren't actually adding to my knowledge*.

Rather, what they were sharing was distracting me from the things that I needed to be doing. It was a nice distraction, but I couldn't really afford that distraction at the time because I had other shit to do. (Like generate income — hello!)

So I put up all these barriers. I blocked all the inputs and I started focusing exclusively on my own paper.

That move, that placing of boundaries, allowed me to steer pretty clear of comparisonitis. It also allowed my writing to evolve with my own voice because I wasn't reading other people's stuff and then accidentally imitating them. And my website is still pretty simple because I haven't been sitting here feeling bad about myself for not having a website like Marie Forleo. I don't care, *because it does what it's supposed to do*. Clients find me and know quite quickly if I'm the right fit.

Information bias

The Misconception: *If I read all the things, I'll succeed!*

The Truth: *Increasing your volume of information or knowledge will not lead to greater success. It will lead to cognitive overload and, in many cases, inertia.*

It's all about need-to-know versus nice-to-know, and what you do with the knowledge you have.

I mean, just because you know what you need to do to be fit, does that mean that you're actually fit? Because I've gained five kilos in the past month and a half, even though I know how to be fit. I know what the steps are to get fit. And yet, I'm not getting more fit.

And so just because you're learning all this stuff about business doesn't mean anything's going to happen, because an idea without action is nothing. It's synaptic electricity. That's it.

The only thing that you need to know is what you need to do right now, today.

So if you're thinking, "Oh I'm trying to build my list, but I want to launch a course so I should take this thing about launching." Don't do it, Benjamin! You're not launching a course until four to six months from now and if it's not relevant right now, today, this week, you should not be consuming it. It is only going to take up valuable headspace, which is really unwise. It's counterproductive. It's an excuse. It's resistance to doing The Work that needs to be done right now.

So how do you know what you're about to sign up for or consume is something you legitimately need to learn now? Easy: when you have a task directly in front of you that you need to implement and you don't have the data that you need.

For example, when I was planning the community project I was thinking, "OK. I know that I need to be doing the legwork in November and December in order for it to happen in January. Therefore, I need to talk to someone in October so they can tell me what legwork is required so that I'm ready to put it into action."

The things I need to learn right now are concrete and immediate with defined results.

These are not nice-to-know pieces of information for the future of my business. It's "I need to know this now in order to execute the next steps."

I know it's tempting to learn what you think you'll need, but you *can't contingency-plan eternity*. That's what most people are inadvertently doing when they get caught up in information bias. "What if one day I want to run Facebook ads? I need to take a course now so I'll know what to do!" No you don't, Sandra. Cross that bridge when you get to it, mmkay? Being preemptively reactive is wasting away the genius work you could be doing right now.

Emotional contagion

The Misconception: *What people tell you about your chances of failure or success is true.*

The Truth: *While it's easy to get caught up in the emotions of the language you've surrounded yourself with ("You'll never make it" or conversely "I did this and so can you!"), this does not have to have any bearing on whether you will actually fail or succeed with your ideas.*

"If I can do it, so can you." This catchy concept is how nearly all the Internet marketers sell their shit.

"Here's my six-figure method. I did it and I'm a copywriter just like you!"

It's pretty, packaged success.

Here's the thing: We are not all the same. Nobody's just like you. That's where the *lie* is and why emotional contagion can be such a serious cognitive trap.

We are really fucking complex human beings. As my super genius friend Randi Buckley says, we must always employ "context, nuance, and discernment."

We are not all at the same stage, not from a business-development perspective nor psychologically. Most of the time we're in completely different stages of the game from the people that we're learning from or comparing ourselves to.

Not to mention, we're surrounded in our nuclear (offline) lives by dramatically different people. And this goes back to the stakeholders element I wrote about in Chapter 8. Nobody has the same stakeholders around them. We're all fielding different inputs.

Whether you're an entrepreneur or an artist or a creative or whatever, you're bringing things out into the world. You're turning your ideas into things. Hello, how cool is that? It's a superpower. And the people around you, the *energy around you* is greatly going to affect your decisions. It's 100% true.

And so the people that are building you up or tearing you down in your immediate sphere...the bandwagons that you're jumping on based on the groups that you're in online or in person...that matters *a lot*.

People who have achieved a modicum of success will often suggest that it's key to have a tight-knit group of smart entrepreneurs to brainstorm with because they can really make or break your business. The key is having people who are as smart as you (or smarter) that *get you*. Their mission, their ethics, their values are in alignment with yours. Naturally, when you surround yourself with those kinds of people, your work and impact will dramatically shift — in a good way.

People get lost in the early stages *because* of the emotional contagion and NLP language used in marketing. It's the "We're all going to make a million dollars if we all join this awesome Facebook group and do Facebook ads!" folly. They mistake that for the thing that I'm talking about, which is a much deeper connection and much greater resonance that goes well beyond emotionally hyped-up tactics. Now, this isn't to say that you don't need groups around you, or that you should lone wolf it out. It is extremely important to have a great group of people around you, but this type of bullshit is not that. I'll talk more specifically about developing your peer group in Chapter 12, so just put a pin in this concept for a bit.

Hyperbolic discounting + omission bias

I'm going to run through two final traps that are not so much "This is how your brain will trick you, because you are human" but more "This is dumb, don't do that."

The other cognitive traps are sort of more built into our human character, but these you can actually skip over if you're aware of them.

The first one is hyperbolic discounting: choosing a smaller reward sooner instead of waiting for a bigger reward. This is the temptation to invest in things that have a short-term payoff when really I need a big long-term one, which requires patience. Shiny object syndrome meets instant gratification.

Examples?

- Spending a bunch of cash on promoting a low-cost offer to a cold audience and getting a good volume of buyers but who have very little loyalty and are only buying your thing because it feels like a deal. Fooled into thinking that selling lots of widgets in a launch is great, without realizing that the long-term value of those buyers may be close to nil.

- Joining a high-end mastermind for a shitload of money thinking that you'll come out the end of that six months or a year with your business rocking (ahem, rarely happens) and bringing home the bacon.

- Taking on clients who aren't right for you because you want the cash, *right now*, and ending up not having capacity to take care of the people who are actually right for you and will stick around long term.

It's a novice's trap, and you learn your way out of it.

And then we have omission bias, or FEAR: False Expectations Appearing Real. This is when you get stuck in the trap of being so afraid to fail that you do nothing. And to be honest, I suspect a good 99% of humans suffer from this. It's the thought process that goes like, "If I don't do anything, I can't fail and therefore I won't get hurt."

Omission bias comes from an inflated sense of consequences, and an inflamed sense of how painful said consequences will be.

If you go back to the olden times (FYI I love that term for talking about pretty much any time pre-1899), this was especially relevant because it was just so much easier to *die*. From everything. Literally. I mean hey, the flu was a real home-wrecker.

But I've talked you through risk and risk perception at length, so you know that your monkey mind's omission bias is nothing to take seriously. Oh it'll pop up. That's a guarantee. And when it does, you can see it, feel it, and *move around it*.

Because guess what's the best way to get past this? Exposure therapy! I know, it sounds a bit perverse, but I promise it has nothing to do with trench coats and nudity. It just has to do with taking small risks and seeing for yourself how inconsequential and non-painful the results are, just like we did with practicing decision-making.

How does the quote go? "Life is inherently risky. There is only one big risk you should avoid at all costs, and that is the risk of doing nothing." Good old Denis Waitley wisdom. And then there's this Steve Jobs quote: "Knowing you have nothing to lose, you are already naked."

The good news is you don't have to worry too much about these final traps because once you spot them, you can't unsee them. Once you know they're bound to pop up in your headspace, you'll be able to see them for what they are and move around them a lot faster.

Awareness is everything.

Well young Padawan, you have now faced your own biases and

gotten a crystal-clear understanding of the most common cognitive traps for incurable entrepreneurs. Congratulations! You've achieved [Scientology level something]. Just kidding. No culty status levels around here.

Now you can have fun confronting and working around these traps. I'm tellin' ya...this is what separates the good from the great. And even if this isn't your idea of fun, you can rest assured that you'll now be dodging bullets that so many of your peers are being taken out by on a daily basis. You're way ahead of the game if you internalize the content of this chapter. Which is awesome.

As I've said before, the biggest barrier to success is between your own two ears. Yes, there are institutionalized barriers and varying degrees of privilege accessible to different people, but in the end, the final barrier will always be your own damn self. So let's work on that, OK?

Next: decision-making, hooray!

Decision-Making

PUT.
ON.
YOUR.
SEATBELT, FRIEND.

Because we're about to dive into probably *the* most game-changing concept in this book. It's the most tangible, use-it-every-second-of-your-entrepreneurial-life tool: decision-making.

Sure, it sounds pedestrian. *Boring* even. But take a sec to think about how much paralysis you've suffered from due to an inability to make a decision. Big decisions, small decisions...we struggle because we have human brains, and the human brain is not a naturally gifted decision-maker in the modern age. Yeah, that's right. Here's your permission to stop beating yourself up about not knowing what to do.

We're wired to stay safe.

We're wired to be a bit myopic. We're wired to think in more black-and-white terms.
This or that.
Safety or uncertainty.
Known outcomes (familiar) or unknown possibility (unfamiliar = scary!).

Let me give you a low-level example.

Decision presented: Should I try this vegan burrito with the delicious-sounding cashew nut paste even though I'm not vegan? Or should I stick with the delicious sweet potato and steak burrito that's a hit every time?

Result: Due to my hatred of food disappointment, I'm probably going to stick with tried and true and, as such, never know how goddahmb delicious the vegan one is.

Familiar. Safe. Also: boring, non-expansive, small. Brain wins, but brain doesn't know what's best, so *I have to override the programming.*

And when you expand the decision-making beyond something that only affects you, like what you're going to put in your mouth for dinner, there's a whole other layer of resistance that kicks in because we're terribly afraid of the responsibility of our decisions. We don't want to disappoint other people. We don't want to be the one to carry the blame. Whether it's something small like recommending a pizza place that your group of friends ends up being underwhelmed by, or being at the helm of a $10k app that flopped...we don't want to be *that guy*. Understandably! It sucks, right?

No word of a lie, my entire 20s was a series of conversations that went something like,

"What do you want to eat?"
"IDK, what do you want to eat?"

I'm going to repeat this subtle reframe again: It's not that we're terrible at decision-making. It's that we're afraid of carrying the responsibility of the decision.

And the uber-shitty fallout of this fear is that — and I'm not using hyperbole here — *we miss out on our dreams.*

That's why honing the skill of making better decisions is *such* a critically important tool.

Bad decisions, best-case scenario, are a waste of time. Worst-case scenario, they cost you lots of money, spirit, or face. But it's nothing you can't (1) prep yourself for nor (2) recover from. Like I say, if no one has died or lost a limb, it's going to be fine.

As an entrepreneur, most decisions are all on you. And that's a lot of responsibility. So how do you get over that? There are many smart tools to help you level up, but the long and the short of it is to default to the scientific method. Meaning, think about decision-making in terms of data.

Make an input, get an output, process the data.

It sounds really rudimentary and I'll elaborate below. But this really is the foundation of all great decision-making.

At all points in time, you're making the best decisions you can with the information you have, even if that information is emotion- or gut-based.

There's a wide spectrum between full risk aversion and deeply confident decision-making. And now is our opportunity to move you along that spectrum so that you can ship more of your work to create the impact you want.

But wait! Remember to be kind to yourself

Humans are naturally risk-averse, so I want you to approach this chapter starting with being kind to yourself.

As someone who has stepped, or is stepping outside the Matrix, you've already proven yourself to be someone who's not house-mouse scared to take a chance. Recognize that every decision is an act of bravery. Most people will never in their lives be remotely as brave as you are. The simple act of being decisive every single day and taking small risks every single day is boss.

And also: give yourself some credit

It's high time we start celebrating our bravery. I think it's a massive shame that we don't do that enough as adults. We don't champion ourselves or others. We're so distracted by big wins like fame, money, social media followings, bestselling books, etc. that we completely fail to celebrate the multitude of small decisions and risks that allow us to achieve those things.

But we need that so badly. The journey is long and we need to see how stepping up to the plate in micro-ways every single day is badass. We need the encouragement. It's not weak to need people to rally behind us. We need the village — we always have.

So I'll start: you fucking rock.

Good on you for hitting send on that ballsy proposal.
Well done on firing that energy-vampire client.
Kudos for making the (slightly-painful-but-it's-over-now) shift to a more structured bookkeeping system.
Mega respect for the way you field scepticism from relatives/neighbours/anyone about what you do for a living and stick to your vision.
Excellent work on closing down your free Facebook group and opening up a high-value paid online community.

Your decisions are shaping your future. Quite literally. So let's dig in and learn how to use that muscle to its greatest capacity.

Decision-making 101

The most important takeaway for me from going through Seth Godin's altMBA program was developing the skill of decision-making. I used to use the bullshit excuse that, "Oh, I'm a Libra, we can't make decisions to save our life." Quite frankly, that's ridiculous. I don't even believe in astrology. The truth was that I couldn't decide because as I referenced previously, *I didn't want to live with the responsibility of the decision.*

Maybe there was a deeper issue here in my case. I had to raise myself from the age of 10, and kids who raise themselves generally have a different relationship to responsibility (it's suffocating) than people who had a more supportive upbringing. Maybe I didn't want to decide because I couldn't handle a single fucking thing more on my shoulders, even if it was what toilet paper to buy. Someone else decide, please! I'm over it!

But when it came to being a full-fledged business-owning adult in my 30s, this pattern wasn't serving me anymore. The pain of staying the same was greater than the pain of change. So change I did. And it was Seth's altMBA program — specifically the introduction to Eisenhower's Matrix, precisely at a time when I needed it — that kicked off a cascade of different thinking and changed everything for me.

Here's Eisenhower's Matrix, filled in with some examples:

	URGENT	NOT URGENT
IMPORTANT	**DO** *Do it now* • Write email newsletter to go out tomorrow • Turn in project to client • Do shitty tax paperwork thing so you make the deadline	**DECIDE** *Schedule a time to do it* • Exercise • Call family and friends • Choose a VA to hire
NOT IMPORTANT	**DELEGATE** *Who can do it for you?* • Schedule interviews • Create invoices • Social media shares	**DELETE** *Eliminate it* • That project that's only sunk costs now • Sorting through junk mail • Filing stuff from last year

I know...this way of looking at things seems pretty simple. Pretty intuitive. But so many of the most simple and intuitive things are freaking hard to do. Take exercise, or not eating too much sugar. Both should be easy, but they're two of the hardest things that we deal with in these somewhat lazy, carb-craving human bodies we have. So why would things like *making logical decisions based on desired endpoints* be any different?

Our brains *fucking looooove* avoiding anything that seems remotely difficult. We're legends at creating false urgency. You know, the old, "I'll just answer these two emails before I sit down to work on the book," which then turns into two hours of faffing about in your inbox with no meaningful progress. Or "Just gotta watch this YouTube clip on how to set up filters in Gmail before I do my taxes." Ugh. Been there a million times. Still go there (let's keep it real).

Rarely do we actually go through the mental exercise of triaging what's urgent and important versus what's not urgent but still important. And even better, what's neither urgent nor important at all but somehow still on our to-do list luring us away from the stuff that matters, taking up precious headspace that we *need* in order to cut through the resistance and focus on what lives in the upper two quadrants.

Eisenhower's Matrix is all about prioritizing what to do next, which is excellent because most small business owners are crap at this in the first few years. So adopting the urgent/important way of thinking early on is a stellar foundational step.

Unfortunately, it's not as useful when you're trying to make bigger, more contextual business decisions. Things like whether or not to invest $5,000 in the execution of a marketing plan isn't an urgent/ important decision so much as it is a more nuanced question of, "Is this what the business needs right now and will it reach the right people?"

This is where the skill of decision-making becomes more of a...well... *skill*. We make decisions based, in part, on data points, right? So it stands to reason that when we're indecisive, it's because we're lacking in data points. But I would posit that this isn't always the case. I've worked with clients for many years who had all the data points but still couldn't make a decision. Why?

I've got four reasons for you, based entirely on my own observations (I'm a coach, not a scientist, Jim!):

1) They didn't trust the data points
2) They didn't trust themselves
3) They were attached to sunk costs
4) They were worried about the outcome, about finding out it was the wrong decision later on

On trusting the data points

OK, so you don't trust the data points. Well, I have some bad news for you: every decision starts with a series of little decisions. If you don't trust the data points, you need to either gather more data points, look for *better quality* data points, or simply trust that what you have in front of you has to be sufficient to inform your decision. That's a mini-decision about making the decision.

It may seem ludicrous that I'm breaking this down with such granularity, but the sheer volume of humans who struggle with decision-making over reasonably inconsequential topics tells me that the breakdown is crucial for many.

Sometimes there is simply no more data available to us and we have to trust what's in front of us. Indecision is no longer an option. Indecision will hurt you and others. It will delay you in getting your work in front of the people who need it.

Let's also put this into a bit of perspective. We're more informed as a species right now than we have ever been in all of history. Being someone who's spent an inordinate amount of time at sea in the polar regions, I often think about the centuries prior when whalers and explorers had almost no data to work with in terms of the weather forecast or sea conditions. And they had no way of knowing what ice conditions would be like once they arrived in Antarctica. Can you imagine being caught in a massive storm on a ship in Antarctica, before engines existed? ("Good luck with your old-timey wooden sailboat, guys!")

I know...it seems a bit random, but the polar regions are a big part of my work life and there were *a lot* of people taking huge risks before the modern era with relatively little data to go on. But they were driven by curiosity, by the insatiable need to forge new ground, to conquer the unknown.

And guys like Shackleton, Scott, and Amundsen did an absolute *shit-ton* of legwork to gather as many data points as they could before attempting journeys that could very easily lead to their death if something went wrong. They tested all of their methods, did shorter practice runs, and chose team members that were super capable and brought something unique to the team that would benefit everyone.

They thought outside the box.

For example, Amundsen had the genius to realize using dogsleds in Antarctica would be way more effective than just a bunch of men pulling heavy sledges full of gear and food.

They iterated based on data gathered.

They were well aware of the unknowns and worked to find answers, and to deal with the unknowns as effectively as possible. This is your job now too.

On trusting yourself

Trusting yourself is like a muscle. You have to exercise it. There's no magic pill that will make you trust yourself more. It's just sheer practice. It's trying and failing until you build confidence in your ability to look at things with a critical, constructive lens.

Trusting yourself fully also requires you to be retrospective. For the times when things didn't work out, why? What didn't you see? What can you be more conscientious of next time? And how do you look back on what you could have done better as a learning exercise without beating yourself up?

Remember that we're all doing the best we can with the tools and data we have at any given time. Having compassion for yourself is a fundamental part of the growth process. It's the ability to say without judgment, "I made the decision at the time based on X, and that made sense. In retrospect, I learned Y and Z, and would choose differently now because I have more data."

On sunk costs

We covered this in-depth in the last chapter so I'll just throw a reminder in here. Being attached to sunk costs is a result of the emotional (and financial) investments you've accumulated in a project. The more you've accumulated, the harder it is to *decide* to abandon the idea or project.

These are some of the hardest decisions to reckon with. And you need to ask yourself whether the investments that got you here — that you feel emotionally beholden to — will help you/your business move forward. Or will you just be throwing good money after bad?

Remember: when we know better, we do better. (Preach, Maya Angelou!)

'Nuff said.

On outcomes

As I mentioned earlier, we often have trouble deciding because we're afraid of living with the responsibility of the outcome. This, dear reader, is the *illusion of control*. You can have all the data in the world guiding your decision, and then something will fly in from left field and fuck it all up. The sooner you can teach yourself to let go of the outcome and rather *go with the flow of experimentation*, the better. You'll at the very least be about 1,094,376 times happier because you won't tell yourself that you're shit every time you don't get the outcomes you expected.

You have no real control. I have no control. We only have predictions and plans. I could get run over by a snowmobile tomorrow (I live in the boonies) and all my best-laid plans would be toast.

There, doesn't that feel lighter?

I wasn't kidding when I said that decision-making is one of the most tangible, use-it-every-second-of-your-entrepreneurial-life tools. Heck, this isn't just an entrepreneurial levelling up. It's a human cognitive evolution that you will be so infinitely grateful for as you grow better at it.

Look, there will always be difficult decisions to grapple with. But the lower-level ones that currently hold you hostage will become so much easier over time, and you'll have way more confidence in tending to the bigger ones.

This is how we become smarter and more strategic with risk-taking. This is how we learn to trust our gut even more. *We're fine-tuning the machine, baby.*

I leave you with this: any time you've got a decision to make, run yourself through the following:

- Do I trust the data points?
- Do I trust myself to make an informed decision?
- Am I holding on to sunk costs here?
- What's the worst that can happen? (I'll have more data when I see the results and can iterate/improve from there.)

Defining Outcomes and Working with Data

MATH AND PLANNING are really not in my wheelhouse of strengths. I mean, *really* not my strengths. Numbers, data, tracking...anything with stats or trends and my brain starts going, "Hmmm, is there any cheese in the fridge? I don't think so. I should probably go to the store and get some cheese just so we have some."

Total-mega-resistance is a light way of putting it. And yet, I'm now going to take you down this critically important rabbit hole: the skill of defining outcomes and working with data. (Breathe, Lynn. You can do this.)

Of course, if you're a data nerd, hats off to you! I am ENVIOUS! You are my hero. But for the rest of you, this isn't a section you can afford to skip.

There's a reason why successful businesses are successful, and it's not just because they have a product or service that's hit a market sweet spot. It's because they know where they're going with their business growth and they pay attention to market response along the growth trajectory over time. If you sidestep this process, your business will fall into the trap of being *reactive*, and that's never a good thing.

You must know where you're going, and you must pay attention along the way, in order to get the outcomes you hope for.

We've touched on this a little bit before in Chapter 2, where I encouraged you to view everything as an experiment. Now we're going to get into how exactly you do that, and how this skill will totally change your business planning + performance. Sound good?

Why is it important to be able to define outcomes?

Defining outcomes is a critical piece of the puzzle because you're moving your business along a spectrum, and to make that happen, you have to have goals or milestones set up. Otherwise, how do you know what direction you're moving in, what you're moving towards, or whether you're moving at all!?

I would say that lack of defined outcomes to work with is probably one of the death knells of many a business within the first two years. (That and not knowing the bigger-picture fingerprint of your work.)

I've watched so many businesses come into being where a business owner creates a course or service, launches it (to varying degrees of success), and then afterwards the business fizzles for a while *because they're not sure what's next.*

Then they try to launch round two of the course or service but it doesn't get the same traction as the first time, and 18 months later the business owner has pivoted to another industry (FYI: your problems will follow you, so pivoting ain't gonna fix things) or they've gone back to a job.

Defining outcomes isn't as simple as "I want to make $10,000 on this launch." Defining outcomes must involve both hard endpoints like financial targets or enrollment numbers *and* the soft endpoints of where you want your clients or customers to end up after they engage with you or your product or service.

You aren't just hitting targets, you're evolving your whole business along a spectrum. On a sub-level, you're also moving your customers or clients along a spectrum: they're going on a journey as they work with you or buy from you. Without clearly defined steps, neither you nor your customer will understand the transformation that is being offered through the work that you do.

It's worth mentioning that being able to define outcomes helps you avoid both despair and shiny object syndrome. Inevitably, if you don't have defined outcomes, you'll feel like you're just working in your business, throwing things at the wall to see what sticks, and then changing tack and trying something else...spinning your wheels...two steps forward, one step back...forever. With no end in sight. Which feels like total garbage. Believe me, I've been there.

And, same problem — different side of the coin — if you don't define outcomes, then your business feels more volatile and unanchored. And you run the very real risk of giving into shiny object syndrome. Because when you've been working your arse off and not seeing the growth or results you know you *should* be able to achieve, shiny promises on the Internet suddenly look *really* appealing. Like, 25-year-aged-Dutch-gouda-level appealing. (Or, endless-bucket-of-kale-chips appealing for the vegans out there.) But we all know where that gets you: with less money in your bank account and not much closer to the business you feel you should be running by now.

TL;DR: without defining your outcomes you run the risk of feeling like you never accomplish anything of note or get real traction.

"OK, sold. So how do I set good goals?"

This is *such* a good question — and the answer is relatively simple, but nuanced. As much as I like to avoid all things corporate-speak, there is a lot of validity in certain age-old principals, like setting SMART goals. I'm sure you've heard this before, but just in case you've been living under a rock, here's a brief recap.

SMART stands for Specific, Measurable, Achievable, Realistic, and Timely.

If we use launching a course as an example, here's how that might look:

Specific: "I'd like 50 people to sign up."

Measurable: Yep, 50 is a measurable number.

Achievable: Based on a mailing list of 1,000, that's a 5% conversion rate (which is on the high end of the industry standard...you can expect something closer to 2%, depending on the price point of your offer).

Realistic: See "Achievable" above. Is your mailing list highly engaged? Are your price point and the problem you're solving in alignment with exactly what these people need *right now*? If your goal doesn't seem realistic, you may need to adjust "Specific" above.

Timely: Your product or service should either be something that you've primed your audience for (ideal) or that's answering a current market demand. Understanding this, is it timely for the 50 people you want to invite to buy?

Honestly, that's kind of it. Using the SMART approach is the foundation that you should always have in place. And each piece is a non-negotiable. Believe me, if I had a dollar for every time I saw someone ignore the "timely" part of goal-setting and then have their goal completely *flop*, I'd be buying up century homes and refurbishing them for fun.

Of course, you'll want to set a few goals per project using this framework because "number of signups" isn't enough to measure overall success.

Along those lines, there are a couple of nuances we need to discuss. What you don't want is to set your SMART goals with no future vision in place. The point isn't to set goals that only generate revenue or hype, but to enable *growth*.

Short-term vision is thinking, "If I make $20k with this launch, I can put that addition on my deck."

Long-term growth vision is thinking, "If I make $20k on this launch, I'll have X amount to cover my current launch expenses, I'll have X amount of revenue to put into marketing for Y, and X amount to roll into project Z, with X amount left over to pay myself."

It might sound obvious, but planning to *generate revenue which will be earmarked for future marketing initiatives* is not something that all business owners instinctively do. There's no doubt that guesswork is involved, and no outcomes are guaranteed, but what gets measured gets done. What you pay attention to grows.

In other words, if you're not looking at where your current goals are going to feed specific future growth initiatives, there's something (major) missing.

The point here is that you need to know what big-picture goals you've got coming down the road so you can figure out *what you need to do now.*

Honestly, this is a large part of why I get to do what I do. I come in from the sidelines to help people be strategic with their projects and outcomes. Because objectivity is almost impossible to maintain about one's own business, and launching a product or service is — for most people — a psychological hamster wheel from hell!

"Sure, that works for you, Heather. But I know nothing! How can I set a reasonable goal?!"

That's great! No one knows what the hell they're doing in the beginning. That's why being curious is one of the most important traits of entrepreneurship. When you're starting out, even if you're not new to business but just delving into a new area, you're going to be doing a lot of (educated) guesswork. You've got to look at industry standards, understand the factors under your control vs. not in your control, and then try to set SMART goals from there.

Over time, the aim is to shift the ratio of "pulling this out of my ass" to "I've got the data to set a reasonable goal," but when you're starting out, it's entirely possible that you'll just be making something up.

A perfect example of this is way back in 2013 when I launched a course called Kick Comparisonitis. I had almost zero data to go on as to whether people would be interested in taking this six-week course because when I polled my (rather small) mailing list, no one responded. I suspected this was because there was so much shame around admitting to being a victim of imposter syndrome, but I *knew* that it was a real issue because in many of my 1:1 client conversations it came up as a huge barrier.

So, I created the course because I felt it was important, and then crossed my fingers and launched it. I made an educated guess based on anecdotal evidence, but I also kept my expectations humble. I maybe had 350 people on my mailing list at the time, so I was only expecting about five signups, and I got seven. (Exactly 2% conversion!) Hooray! It doesn't sound like much, but it was a great start and a way for me to test my material. It also gave me a lot of data from actual users that helped me make decisions around the product and experience moving forward.

Let's talk about gathering data.

"Eew, Heather, data sounds scary! I'm not a scientist! And what if I look at the data and it tells me that I'm completely wrong in all of my assumptions and my business is about to go up in flames of ignorance?"

I get it. Data is very unsexy for your average creative. It's actually not the data itself, but rather knowing where on earth to start. It's scary because it's unfamiliar. We feel an aversion because we don't *really* know WTF "data" means. What data should we be looking at? How do we get it? And even when we do know, extrapolating next steps based on data can also be really fucking intimidating. Like all non-intuitive things, it feels distressing when we don't understand it. So part of your entrepreneurial journey has to be dipping your toes into data and market research.

Don't worry! Data is your friend, and you don't have to face it alone. You *shouldn't* face things you feel intimidated by alone. Why? Because it'll get ignored (helloooo procrastination!) and you can't afford to ignore this stuff. So harness your network of entrepreneurial brain power, or work with a coach or a mastermind group that has experience tracking data to take the 'scary' out of it.

Furthermore, knowing what data to look for is the key to success here. Otherwise you can get super overwhelmed trying to track a zillion things, or you can track the wrong things and end up with a useless data set.

I've tracked the wrong things a million times in the past. For example, just because someone's on a mailing list doesn't mean they have any interest in buying what I'm selling. I built a large list for our polar expedition company that I thought was interested in higher-end bespoke cruises, but really most of them were more general travellers who were looking for something with a lower price point. Here I was tracking our subscriber data thinking we had a warm list, when we really didn't! (Useless data set — boo!)

It wasn't until I made the opt-in *very* specific that we were able to create a warm list of truly interested buyers who were looking for exactly what we were dishing out. The learning here from the original hiccup really helped us level up to where we needed to be to grow the business.

A couple of reminders here that will help: it's all just a big experiment and *your value* isn't on the table.

Two keys to getting useful data

The first key is to know (or have some idea of) what you're looking for. The simplest way to do this is to look at your goal and then reverse engineer the data points from there. Here we're talking about the "hard numbers" type of data that most people think about when they think about data collection. (AKA, "I want to build my list, so I'm going to track list growth. Obvs.")

Even the act of stating, "I want to grow my list by 1,000 in three months" means you now have to work on getting approximately 333 signups per month (which you can further track weekly to make sure you're on target), and it also means you have to have something salient enough on offer that you'll attract that many people to your mailing list. And then if your offer isn't getting the signup numbers you want after month one, you can try different strategies to increase opt-ins. And remember, *hope is not a strategy*. Likewise, data alone is also not a strategy...but it does point you right towards what you need to focus on!

Along those lines, it's important to mention here how everything you do in your business should be done with a purpose, and therefore should be trackable. "Feelings" are not data points per se — you can't just "feel" like you're more visible and have that be the answer to "Did I or did I not create more visibility?"

The second key — and one of the most overlooked elements — is human data. Buying is a deeply emotional decision, and not some Adam Smith *homo economicus*–type thing. We're not only looking to track signups, clicks, or purchases but the reasons that underlie those. You know, the irrational reasons we buy the course or click out of the sales cart.

Believe me, even the most random, non-emotional purchase has emotion at its root.

Example[11]: I hate flaccid cushions. I really do. Few things seem like such a total waste of money than cushions that *appear* nice when you buy them, but become mushy and lose their integrity within the first couple of months. Don't sell me mushy cushions!

I also can't stand cushion covers that start to pill or look crappy, which has made me — at 41 years of age — an extreme(ly experienced) discerner of cushions. I can see a dud from a mile away.

Lo, I was in South Africa not a month ago visiting my bestie and while at some awesome makers fair I saw a cushion that blew my freaking mind. It had a beautifully designed pattern (apparently it was a custom design for Prince Harry when he paid ZA a visit) and it had *integrity*. I could see that this thing was plush and would hold up over time. It was also a shitload of money, but if I'd had space in my suitcase I would have bought it for sure.

I mean, who buys an obscenely expensive sofa pillow? {Both thumbs point at my face.} This chick does. Because I hate goddahmb flaccid crappy pillows! I'm making an emotional high-ticket purchasing decision here. And the makers of these pillows *know* that people like me exist. They make pillows for the MEs of the world. And some other people of course...like rich people...but their products are clearly for a discerning customer.

So much of gathering the human data is about developing a deep empathy for your audience. As someone selling something, you have to create an environment where they can open up and talk about the

---

11 Spoken like Dwight Schrute when he says, "Question."

things that really matter. And yes, even about cushion integrity. The

woman at the stall selling the cushions could have geeked out with me about cushions for a good hour. She *got* me.

On the flip side, we were in the market to buy a house about six months ago and I keenly remember being at a property for a viewing when I asked the agent what year the geothermal heating unit was installed and he was like, "I dunno, check the brochure." He was so disinterested in the thing he was selling and, even worse, wholly disinterested in the emotional experience of potential buyers.

You do not want to be one of those people who's like, "I dunno, check the brochure."

We are humans, selling things to humans. Our success depends in large part on our curiosity and empathy as we look for the data needed to find the intersection between what we're putting out and what others are looking for.

A lot of this is about feeling into the data as a whole — getting a sense of the overall trends. Because we're dealing with humans, it's naturally going to be a little messy and involve a little guesswork. But as you seek deeper and deeper empathy, the more you'll get a feel for things.

Here's one way I like to think of it: you're on a path, and your audience is on a path, and you're looking for ways to make those paths intersect. Kind of like a helix: you and your customers connect and then move apart, connect and move apart. The better you understand yourself and your people, the more often and more appropriately you can make those helices intersect.

Side note! Everyone fucks it up, and you will, too.

I've said it before and I'll say it again: every single person gets this wrong now and again. Maybe more often than not. It's just data, and ultimately this is just a big experiment, and that's why it's really important not to attach yourself to outcomes.

But also be wary not to get so overconfident that you think, "Every time I create something, gold shoots out my ass!" You can never be 100% sure. You can do all the research in the world and you might still get it wrong. And that's totally OK because it's just a bump in the road.

Not to mention, every time you get it wrong or you're slightly off course and things don't work out the way that you thought...those are often the most insightful times. You'll see where you've completely missed *this* element or *that* blind spot. You'll see the assumptions that you made because you've been doing this for a while. And then you recalibrate.

Two really important reminders

OK, we've made it this far but we've got two final things to talk about when it comes to data.

First, never assume all data points are true. I get examples of messages from readers in my inbox occasionally — *even though I know better* — that give me pause.

My brain: "Wait...why is this guy emailing me? He's not even close to my ideal client...IS MY MESSAGING ATTRACTING THE WRONG PEOPLE?? AHHH!!! Fuck...now I have to reassess all my web copy..."

And then I take a deep breath and remind myself that it's *one* data point. I mean, my book editor is also a highly acclaimed copywriter, and she gets people pitching her with offers of a web copy overhaul. *Like her copy isn't good enough.* WTF?!? Stuff like that is an irrelevant data point. And you've gotta watch out for those suckers because they can derail even the most confident and seasoned businesspeople.

A huge part of this is developing discernment to see the trends and the bigger picture, and that's a skill that takes time. It's also *really smart* to get an outside opinion on data points that seem confusing, incongruent, or even emotionally derailing (a la, "I didn't think your course offered anything new").

I recently had someone from my mailing list write me an email about how invasive and weird it was that my newsletters address readers by their first name. She stated that while she enjoyed my newsletters, we were not personal friends, and she felt it was very off-putting. I thought, "Meh...irrelevant data point." I know pretty much all of my other readers like this feature *and* there's plenty of data proving that personalizing communications is smart marketing. It creates a more familiar connection between you and the readers you are hoping will choose to do business with you. It's a shame that one of my readers doesn't like it, but it's also not my problem. There's a bigger picture here that I'm serving.

Secondly, do not rest on your laurels. (Imagine that stated out loud in Alan Rickman's voice. It makes you pay attention, right?) Your relationship with and interest in data collection around your business needs to be a living, ongoing process (and in fact, the easiest way to fuck up is to stop and use old data).

This doesn't mean you have to collect #alltheinfo forever — some things are going to be naturally time-bound, like a launch or a course, in which case you'll need to be more responsive to the data in real time for the duration of said project. But data collection and insight related to other things, like your relationship with your clients or readers or community, is going to be ongoing as long as you're in business.

That's a lot.
And that's hard.
And that's the job.

It's a relationship, not some sort of "figure out how to hack the slot machine that is the Internet" dude-bro bullshit.

In the relationship economy, you're in relationship with both your business and your customers. These relationships are long-term endeavours. If you recognize that and tend to them, you'll be rewarded significantly.

Stakeholders and Peers

WELL DONE, FRIEND. You made it through the data chapter! It was a bit like surviving the Fire Swamp from *The Princess Bride*, no?

Buttercup: We'll never succeed. We may as well die here.

Westley: No, no. We have already succeeded. I mean, what are the three terrors of the Fire Swamp? One, the flame spurt — no problem. There's a popping sound preceding each; we can avoid that. Two, the lightning sand, which you were clever enough to discover what that looks like, so in the future, we can avoid that too.[12]

The moral? If you know what you're getting into and you're proceeding with eyes wide open, you'll be just fine. (#dataisnavigational)

---

12 Wondering about the third terror?
Buttercup: "Westley, what about the R.O.U.S.s?"
Westley: "Rodents of Unusual Size? I don't think they exist." *Immediately, an R.O.U.S. attacks him.*

Now we're about to get into something much less intimidating (though equally important): dealing with your inner circle.

OK, so maybe it's *differently* intimidating. :)

Your inner circle are your stakeholders and peers. By stakeholders, I don't mean investors in the more traditional business sense. I mean people who have a stake in your life and well-being, which goes beyond those directly involved in your business. And your peers are those you surround yourself with as a business owner.

Why is this a thing?

"Heather, I'm an entrepreneurial lone wolf! A *solo*-preneur. I don't need *people*. If I wanted people I'd get an office job that required pants."

I know, I know. I kicked and screamed a bit too. Until the lonely echo of my screams and my dwindling bank account made me realize I was missing the plot. *I needed people.*

Truth: The people already in your life (stakeholders) and the people you surround yourself with as a business owner (peers) are the second most influential elements of your success. (The first element is YOU, obviously.)

This is critical to remember.

We don't do business in a vacuum. If you worked in a job prior to now, you didn't do the job in a vacuum with no one else around. There were other people involved in your work at the office or workplace. There were people who helped you succeed (or not). There were people who managed different pieces of the business. And now when it's just you...are you going to do all of the sales, marketing, bookkeeping, forecasting, and actual service or product delivery?

You can't do something 100% solo.

It's ridiculous. And *even if* your business is lean and you can manage the logistics as a one-person show, you'll need — at the very least — psychosocial support. Because honey, this shit is tough.

What do you do when you have a personal crisis like a breakup or a health scare? You call up your friends. You call up your mom. You lean on other people to help you get through difficult times.

So who are you going to do that with when your business feels like a big dumpster fire? Enter: your peer group. You're going to need smart people who are *aligned with your values*, who *get your business* and the world you run in (i.e., probably not your mom), so that they can talk you off the ledge on the days where you're ready to burn this shit to the ground.

Managing the relationships in your personal life — with your stakeholders — is just as important for running a successful business as anything else. For example, a great partner might lift you up and give you all the support you need in your entrepreneurial journey (huge bonus), while a less supportive partner, someone who's metaphorically tapping their watch and wondering when you're going to "make it" because they never really bought into this "working for yourself thing" to begin with, can make things feel a helluva lot harder.

Stakeholders, good and bad

We're going to start with the stakeholders in your life — they're people who you care about and who are affected by you being in business for yourself. So, that's your partner, parents, kids, your closest friends, siblings, etc.

No, they're not going to be your customers (usually), but your well-being affects their well-being because we're social creatures. These relationships can be a hugely positive force. These people may be the ones supporting you early on before you really know what the fuck you're doing. Aaaand they can also be a negative, with loved ones diminishing your dreams, doubting your capability, or just.not.getting. it. AT ALL.

Your first order of business here is to figure out who these people are for you. Grab a piece of paper and list your core stakeholders and how you being in business will affect them. See if you can get a sense of who your supporters and detractors will be. (Even well-meaning detractors are detractors!) And see if you can get a sense of *how their reactions are going to affect you.*

Think things like:

"Will my parents being upset about me not having the 'security of a paycheck' totally throw me?"

"Am I really hung up on my friend's approval?"

"If my partner doesn't believe in my dream, how am I going to react to that?"

For the stakeholders who you know have your back, keep them in the loop. Share your wins. *Let them know how much their support means to you.* Because truly, this kind of encouragement is priceless when you need it most.

NO PLAN B   261

Sometimes on a super shitty day when I feel really low, my husband will say — with 100% sincerity — something like, "You're the smartest, most resilient person I've ever met. You could take on the world if you wanted to! But come here and let me hug you. What should I cook you for dinner?" I swear to god, no balm is sweeter on a weary entrepreneurial soul than being seen and having someone help carry your load.

But I'm not going to lie. If you have people in your inner circle who don't believe in you or your business, you'll find it reallllyyyyyyy hard to do this work. Not impossible, but tough. And I encourage you to set boundaries and manage your energy around these people because no one — not even a loved one — should come in the way of you doing what you feel called to do.

If you're surrounded by cheerleaders and people who'd roll up their sleeves in a heartbeat to help you build your dream, you are so lucky. Run with that!

But for those of you who have a Debbie Downer (or three) in the mix, here are a couple of tips for managing the detractors:

1) Set boundaries. If you find that certain people default to saying things about your business that make you feel deflated, tell them that conversation is off the table.

2) Understand that some people just won't get it, and that's OK. *You don't have to prove anything to them.*

3) Take the good intentions offered, and leave the rest behind. Sometimes loved ones say things that come from a good place but make you feel, quite frankly, like shit. Knowing that they mean well and letting the rest slide is sometimes your best option.

4) Remember that above all else, this is *your* thing, and you don't have to prove anything to anyone. *You only have to believe in yourself*, and as long as there's one more person out there in the ether who believes in you, then fuck everyone else. {Raises hand...} I believe in you!

And finally, need some "detractor one-liners" to get through holiday meals or that monthly Zoom chat?

Here you go:

"I appreciate your concern, but this is my decision."

"If you don't have anything helpful to offer, I'm not engaging in this conversation."

"I understand you're worried about my financial security, but ~~I'm a grown-ass adult~~ you didn't raise me to be irresponsible."

"What I need now is your support, not your judgment."

"I know this isn't the easy route, but it's the one that's right for me and I ask that you respect that."

The other side of the relationship coin: developing your peer group

There's a reason people tend to come up together in groups. We need the support, we need each other as resources, and we need to be around someone who fucking gets us.

Nobody can manage everything in an entrepreneurial enterprise by themselves. No one can build an asset worth owning without help. And therefore, one of the most important things you can do as a business owner is to develop your peer group.

You absolutely need kindred spirits. You need people who are in your zone, who move in similar circles, who understand the slings and arrows...and as such are *just* the people that can help propel you forward.

Let's look at the example of professional athletes. If you're a pro athlete trying to get to the best you can be — aiming for the best outcomes — are you surrounded by people who have beer guts, eating potato chips on the sofa? No, you're surrounded by people *who get you*, who get the world that you exist in, who get the difficulties and the nuances of being a professional athlete and what that means about every element of your waking hours.

It's no different for entrepreneurs. I know we think of pro athletes as "elite" but we are *pro businesspeople*. We are elite in our own way. We are a part of the first generation of digital entrepreneurs. That's pretty fucking special. We're part of the vanguard that's breaking new ground by moving our livelihoods into the virtual sphere for the first time in history, and we need people around to rally us. We need community, we need coaches...we need all the help we can get.

Back in 2011 when I started working for myself, I was a part of some groups online that were all about building online businesses. It was still the early days of this becoming a thing that people could actually do for a living. I knew from the get-go that there was no plan B for me. I knew self-determination was my future. And so I was pretty hesitant to jump on any bandwagons. I wanted to build thoughtfully for the future.

I was also quietly watching from the Internet sidelines to see who was really worth their salt. Who was truly on top of their craft and even more importantly, who showed the signs of being in this for the long game as well. In other words, my people.

Most of them were like me at the time, not super known on the Internet, just trying to figure things out, and in the process endeavouring to build a body of work that mattered.

We made connections.

Some connections were of convenience or through a preexisting community or working group, but the connections that I still have today (with people who have become hugely more successful than me no less!) are the ones that I knew in my gut way back when would still be here in 2020 rocking the world with their stuff.

I knew it not only because of the way they spoke about their work, the way they made decisions about their business, and the level of integrity they displayed, but also because they were generous and supportive. They were generous and supportive even then they were unknowns and busting their asses as much as I was to get traction with their ideas. And they are still dear friends today.

The key when you're trying to find your people isn't to find fancy people and hang around in their orbit. It's to find people you like who are doing cool shit and then support each other to succeed. Find the people who you can evolve with.

I can't stress enough how important it is to try to find *your* people specifically. The Internet's a big place, and it's easy to think that the first few groups you get involved in are just "how it is" out there, but there really is a place for everyone.

At the time of this writing, I've been in business online for nine years and it was only a few months ago that I was invited into a Facebook group that *I actually like,* that's full of actual professional non-woo-woo women who are doing amazing things in their life and work, sharing ideas and resources, and it's entirely free of bullshit! It's 21,000 people strong and it's a joy to be in there. Nine years. It took me nine years of actively engaging in the online sphere to find a free online group that didn't make me roll my eyes.

Don't worry, it's not going to take you that long. Things are very different now than they were in 2011. But as you look to develop a peer group, this is the time to really own your shit, and let your true self show, because that's how you're going to find your people.

We look for resonance.

I really can't emphasize this enough. People think they have to present a certain way or be Entrepreneur Barbie or whatever, but it's really, really not so. That's like buying a ticket straight to one-hit-wonder-land (because remember, being not-you is not sustainable!) and it'll leave you feeling disingenuous and lonely.

Are you currently in some groups or course communities that seemed good in the beginning but kinda got spammy or woo or just...no? It's absolutely critical that you're willing to cut and run from any space that's not a fit for you. And beware the squeaky wheels! Beware the idea stealers with flash websites and loose ethics. Beware the "can I pick your brain" folks and the wantrepreneurs...oh, the wantrepreneurs...it's common for communities to get overrun with these types. Don't let them steal your mental bandwidth! Get thee out of there.

Look, wherever you're hanging out, just keep an eye out for the people *who do seem like your people.* And then reach out and connect.

Because eventually, you may want to leave the group but maintain those relationships, or you'll find enough of your people and you'll all leave together.

The nuts and bolts of developing a peer group

The good news is that as far as actually, logistically finding people, you can connect with anyone. The Internet makes it waaaaayyyy easy to get in touch with people, and most are very friendly. So if someone seems super interesting, reach out.

Otherwise, hang out in well-managed Facebook groups, follow people on Instagram, engage genuinely on Twitter or Linkedin, etc. And if you already know some cool friends online, ask them, "Who do I need to know?"

Finding your peer group is kind of like moving to a new neighbourhood. You try things out, you show up in places you think will be cool, and you look for people who seem interesting. This is *not* about being weirdly strategic and "networking" your way to success. It's about relationships. It's about really listening to what people are saying and doing, and being discerning.

In the past few years, I've randomly reached out to some people that I've "known" online for years — some almost a full decade — and asked for a virtual coffee date. Not because I want something specific, but because I've seen enough of them that I know they're good people with interesting businesses, and we share the same values. And it's been awesome to connect with these people *every time*. They're like my peripheral business community that I can call upon or refer people to. But it took time for us to really sniff each other out. There's no fast track for this. It really does takes time, and dumb luck, and happy coincidences to find your people.

Conversely, lots of people may want to be in your peer group, but it doesn't mean you want to be in theirs! You've gotta follow your instincts. If you start swimming in the same circles with someone and they just don't feel right, no worries. Move on. If you start hanging around with people and they just don't get you, that's fine too. Someone else will. The whole point is to be as *you* as possible and to trust your instincts, and be patient. Do that, and Your People will appear.

Developing Your Offer

AND JUST LIKE THAT, we're at the final chapter. Though it's the end, *you're now more primed to begin than most.*

I know you may not be new to running a small business, but there are many stages in this journey when you'll press the reset button and *begin again*, or finally step into the bigger-picture work you've been skirting around. I hope you feel re-energized and ready AF.

So. You've thought through all of the foundational pieces and done the internal work, and now we can talk about developing your offer. But before we go there, I'm going to zoom the lens out for just a minute and remind you where we've been.

We started out in the very beginning talking about the Matrix, and how fucked up it is. How once you see the structure for its extractionary nature, inhumanity and divisiveness, you can't unsee it. And you sure as shit can't imagine going back.

We talked about the new world, the world we incurable entrepreneurs are working on making. We covered what's possible when we ignore the old rules and make our own new ones built around relationships, compassion, and inclusion in a humans-first approach. (And that healthy profits aren't exclusive to an extractive economy.)

We then talked about risk, and *seriously* redefined our relationship with it. This is a critical piece, as being an entrepreneur will require you to face higher levels of risk than you ever thought before. I urge you to reread Chapter 2 as much as you need in order to evolve your relationship to risk because it ain't something that happens overnight.

And then we talked about the relationship economy. How business is becoming more and more personal, consumers are looking for more resonance and respect from those they buy from, and about the true stakes of running your business. It's not just to make a great life for yourself — though that's a huge part of it and most people's primary driver.

It's to make a difference.

To DO something, to LEAVE something memorable and better than you found it.

It's to have shipped work that made *each day worthwhile*.

Of course, to do that, you have to really own your own shit. So we spent a couple of very deep, possibly slightly terrifying chapters on getting over yourself, figuring out your reasons for doing this work, understanding your cognitive load, and learning how to game your system.

With all that under your belt, you could then start doing what you need to do to become the entrepreneur you want to be. So we talked through the skill sets that most people only ever stumble their way into after years of entrepreneurship. We talked about cognitive traps, decision-making, defining outcomes and working with data, and the importance of your relationships with stakeholders and peers.

And now, finally, we're getting to the place where most entrepreneurs start: developing your offer.

Say what?! People just start here?

I mean, just take a minute to look back over all that hard work you've done and think about what you have at your disposal now: a clear compass, a grounded sense of self, and a super solid grasp of strategy and tactics. Now imagine you have *none* of that. That's how most entrepreneurs approach offer development.

Without any of the foundational work, you create offers you *think* are good...except you're so hung up and not over your shit that they aren't true to you and they don't sell or you end up hating them. You create offers based on fear and scarcity that flop and leave you deflated after having wasted a lot of time. You've probably experienced this or seen it happen with other business owners. *Because it's common.*

Worst-case scenario, you create offers that aren't grounded in what you actually want to do, so even if they do succeed you end up hating it, or they're a flash in the pan.

Example[13]: I knew a business owner years ago who created an awesome online training program — a program I was in and learned a ton from — and who became really well-known. Everyone talked about her

---

13 Dwight Schrute's voice again.

course because she really filled a niche in the market at the time, and she made a shitload of money running it. We're talking visit-Branson's-island level of cash. (That's not a metaphor, she went to his island.)

But at some point, she realized that while she *could* teach this stuff, she wasn't interested in it anymore. In fact, it wasn't even close to what she wanted to spend her time doing. So she hired some people who had the right skills to do some of the teaching and community management for her...but because her heart wasn't in the material, she started letting things slide. At least one launch happened in which promises of new content — content people had paid for — never materialized. Her community of students started to feel neglected. Communication with the folks she'd hired became more sparse and they felt completely hung out to dry. Eventually, she just abandoned ship and it was *ugly*.

A short while later she resurfaced saying she had found her calling as a spiritual advisor of sorts. She had a new persona, a new website...she'd fully pivoted into something distinctly different.

The clincher is that all of that authority capital she'd built up with her first iteration of online business had been lost. And I honestly have no idea what happened next but I can tell you that within a fairly short period of time she had completely disappeared off the Internet. I mean...nada. She is gonzo and it's been a few years now.

Here's my take: there was likely no unique fingerprint (or an unrefined version of it) backing the first iteration. And the first iteration was successful because it met an immediate market need, which led to a false sense of confidence. (Remember, we just talked about this in Chapter 11 — incorrect data can make you overconfident.) Then she shifted into something completely different, something perhaps unvetted, thinking that everyone would come running, but they didn't.

This is a perfect example of why *all the work you've done* is so important. It empowers you to approach your next evolution with eyes wide open.

A parallel example from within the Matrix is someone who spends a couple of hundred grand and X number of years of their life getting a law degree, starts practicing law, and then goes, "Oh wait, I fucking hate being a lawyer." They're 30 years old, $200k in debt, and the last thing they want to do is practice law.

More and more we hear stories of people coming to the realization that the career path they've invested in is not the one they want. So they ditch it and become a paramedic or a monk[14], or they open up a plastic-free grocery store in Portland. And it's really fucking cool to see people throwing sunk costs to the wind in order to follow their heart.

I believe we need to give ourselves the same permission in the small business world. If you do go down one road — even if you go whole-hog and everybody knows you for *that thing* you do — and then suddenly you're like, "Nope!" that's OK. But...BUT please, please, please be *intentional* about those next steps, vet your ideas, *understand thyself*, and temper your expectations, because chances are you'll be starting from scratch.

How to develop an offer

OK, even if you've been-there-done-that when it comes to offer development, I encourage you to stick with this next exercise because

---

14 I actually know someone who was a lawyer, then became a monk, and then a paramedic. I met him when he was living in Peru working for a travel company after deciding being a paramedic wasn't for him.

nuance is everything, and we become experts by doing things over and over again until we've mastered the art.

I'm going to walk you through the four steps for developing an offer that you can actually, usefully understand and work with and *practice*, because you're so far ahead of 99.9% of other entrepreneurs in the game.

First, you've got to go back to the vision you came up with in Chapter 5. Ask yourself: What's the unique fingerprint I bring to my work, and the lasting imprint I want it to have? Remember that entrepreneurship is the medium for expressing this vision, so your offer needs to be in line with it.

In my work, I want to *create transformational experiences* that help people by *leveraging my superpowers* of ideation and bigger-picture visioning. Sounds totally woo-woo but bear with me. With my current foundational offer for 1:1 clients — the Mastermind Sessions — I spend two days with a client workshopping through all of the elements that make them tick on a personal level, all of the skills they bring to the table, the work they've done up to that point in time, and we lay it all out on the table...kinda like Legos.

Then we piece things together using their unique fingerprint as the compass. We pull together a business plan that both honours and supports the impact they want to create, how they want to work/show up on a regular basis, and the financial and lifestyle goals they have. I get to come in with my ideas and bigger-picture visioning to shine a light in areas my clients are blind to because they're too close to it. I get to show them *what's possible* as we piece the puzzle of their business together and lemme tell you...*I never get tired of this*. It is POWERFUL work for me and it's transformational for my clients. Also, they walk away with a plan that feels both deeply resonant and doable.

Your turn: What kind of offer can hold to your unique fingerprint and allow you to leverage your superpowers at the same time?

Second, you've got to think about what you hate. What ways of working with people do you really not enjoy? What drives you crazy in your industry? What do you think is *wrong* in the world? There's often room to create an offer in that because that, friends, is a fucking pain point, and if you can solve it and make everyone happier, so much the better.

A couple of examples to illustrate this: what drives me crazy in my industry is people peddling formulas. So I don't do it. I customize my coaching to each client and help them make decisions that are true to their vision based on sound business principles. Funny that that makes me an outlier! But I'll take it.

In terms of ways of working with people, I'm not a hand-holder. I can't stand it. So the very structure of my offer respects that I like to dive deep and then let my clients fly. Admittedly, most of my clients then start working with me on retainer...but the key is that I *don't offer the retainer option unless I know the client is driven and independent.* If we do the Mastermind Sessions and I can see the client would need hand-holding moving forward, I know I'm not the right coach to help them implement the business plan we devise for them and I refer them to someone who's a better fit for the next steps.

These are the kinds of very personal leanings you need to be thinking about here when it comes to what you can't stand in the context of creating an offer.

Your turn: What do you really NOT want to creep into your offer? How can you breathe your boundaries or values into the structure of how you deliver your products or services?

Third, you've got to think about how you want to live/work/be. What do you want *your experience of your business* to be like? How much of your time will it require? How will you stay engaged in your work and plan to avoid burnout? This is going to directly inform your business model, and your offer. If you hate being on Facebook all the time, building a Facebook community is probably not the way to go. If you're wildly introverted and don't ever want to talk to people, opening a co-working space may not be your deal. You must get clear on your orientation towards certain types of activities and ways of showing up. There is no right or wrong, but there is the answer that's true for you.

You've already laid a lot of groundwork for this in Section 2 of the book, so let's look at how this plays out in an actual business scenario.

Want to build an online community? Before you start making it a reality, watch other business owners you respect and how they're building similar communities to see what you can learn and what pitfalls to avoid.

I know that one entrepreneur, in particular, started her community from the beginning with other people involved as community managers, which has allowed her to focus on being the owner of the business — and *developing* the business — instead of the person working *in* the business. FYI, this isn't common. More often, community leaders get to the point of being overworked before they bring other people in to relieve them.

This woman very intentionally decided to facilitate a community that has come together around the values that she exemplifies, but she purposely didn't position herself as the centre of the community.

Other people are managing her community, other people are answering questions on behalf of her and her brand, but *she is not required to be in there all the time*, working her buns off on menial tasks. Because that's not her genius zone, and so she built her offer accordingly.

Your turn: How do you want to live/work/be in your business? What does the bigger picture of what you're trying to create tell you about what your role needs to look like?

And fourth, *meet an actual need.* I know it might sound silly to state this but seriously...I'm saying it because I'm so weary of seeing offers like *Create Your Dream Life* coaching!

Your offer needs to meet an actual deep-seated I-will-pay-money-for-this-right-now need. (Yes, including good-quality sofa cushions. This applies to everything!) Here are a couple of guideposts to help you create an offer that doesn't have the personality of day-old oatmeal.

1) If you're a service-based business owner, use the Night Sweats Test. The Night Sweats Test is when you ask yourself, is my ideal customer/client waking up at night fretting over this? Am I offering a solution to the thing that's making them sweaty at 4 a.m.? (This is why it's important you understand what's going on inside your ideal client's mind.)

2) Use the "This is what I've been looking for" Niche Test. Does your product or service make people exclaim out loud to whoever's in the room, "This is what I've been looking for!" (Literally me at the cushion kiosk in Cape Town, BTW.) This is a valid test for either services or products. Just a couple of months ago I was scouring copywriter websites looking for the right fit to overhaul my polar expedition company website copy. When I found the right copywriter, I knew it within the first paragraph on their home page — *this* was what I'd been looking for.

Your turn: What actual need can (or does) your offer meet? I'm making it sound easy but it's incredibly challenging. The actual need under the "I need a copywriter" is very nuanced and is deeply connected to the character of the buyer. Keep that in mind as you play with ideas until you find The Thing that's super resonant.

OK, let's recap:

Your offer should serve and support your bigger vision, and be driven by the unique fingerprint you bring to the table. It should also circumnavigate anything that you hate — clients you don't want to attract, business tasks you're not interested in doing for the long term, etc. Your offer needs to support how you want to live/work/be, avoiding ways of working that don't jive with your preferences or that interfere with your genius work and anticipating the implications of future growth. And finally, your offer needs to meet a real, nuanced, salient need within your target market. Do not be afraid to get specific! Specificity is your competitive advantage.

How to choose between alllll the ideas

Reader, now you're either slow-blinking in overload and not really sure what your offer should be, or you're overflowing with ideas and not sure how to narrow down to the best one. If you fall into the latter camp, look for the sweet spot between skills and excitement.

What does that mean? It means to choose something that you're absolutely fucking awesome at delivering, and that you're equally as excited about engaging with for at least the next few years. What can you do, and what do you *want* to do? What feels exciting and possible? What will you not get sick of anytime soon?

You need to feel excited about it because you'll need the momentum.

When your momentum wanes, the fact that you're awesome at what you do will help you pick yourself up again, because you'll have a pool of raving clients or customers whose energy will bring you back to life.

The important part is to be as honest with yourself as possible here. You'll be tempted to choose the path that appears, in the short term, to be the most financially lucrative. But I promise you that the most financially lucrative one over time will be the one that's still thriving and filling up your energetic cup 3, 5, 10 years down the road. Just like my Mastermind Sessions work with clients: hitting the sweet spot of skills and excitement brilliantly since 2015.

Follow your instincts, and trust in what you've learned and done so far.

And finally, remember...

At the end of the day, this is all an experiment. The stage you're in right now is just one stage, and there are future evolutions to come. So I encourage you to do all the work in this book — even the hard bits — and nail down your offer to the best of your ability using the framework in this chapter. And then just giv'er.[15]

If you go down one road (even really far down) and end up hating it, you can always pivot. Intentionally, right? Right. Though I suspect if you have done the work I've asked you to, you're not going to end up hating any path you choose at this point.

Just stay clear on what the ultimate mission is, and keep people near who can support you and give you objective advice for recalibration when you're down in it.

---

15 One of my favourite Canadianisms.

Above all, it's about action. Act, read the data, adjust accordingly, and repeat.

Congrats, entrepreneur! *You've got this.*

CONCLUSION

Your time is now.

That's the overarching point of this book. Your time is now. Don't be shy. Don't let yourself play small when everything that you could possibly need to bring your ideas to life exists and is mostly free, and you can find the answers and support you need by asking the right questions in the right spaces. And don't fucking give up.

Don't give up, and don't get sidetracked! (Or if you do, that's OK, but just make sure there's someone that can pull you back into the fold.)

Don't do it alone. If you try to do things alone, everything will take 10x longer and be 30x more painful. Why do this to yourself?

This is the time you should be surrounding yourself with people who see your capability, who see your possibility, who won't let you fall off the radar for two or three months because they know how important it is that you show up and you keep working on bringing your ideas to life.

There is no going back now.

If there's no going back, and you have a finite number of days before you die — and we all do, we're all gonna die — with only a finite number of days left, what are you going to do with them?

I remember so clearly sitting in a doctor's office in Toronto during my years as a pharma rep. I had my winter jacket on, because I thought I'd be in and out faster and I wasn't. And I didn't want to take off my jacket for whatever stupid reason because I'm an introvert and I'm weird. So I'm sitting there sweating, and an hour goes by, and I'm reading last year's *Chatelaine*, which I hate, waiting and waiting and waiting to see this fucking doctor, and literally starting to choke back tears.

Because all I could think was, "This is an hour, or now two hours, now two and a half hours, of my life I'm never going to get back. I hate this, I hate being here, I hate this fucking doctor for taking forever. I hate that I'm in this job. I hate that I'm not going to get these hours back.

This is my one sweet life passing before me."

I was so fucking miserable — desperate and resentful — and at the same time, I was so aware that *I was the one who was choosing to be there.*

And, since I left that job, once I left the traditional working world entirely, my whole driving force has been, "I'm not going to let a day go by that was a wasted day."

And I'm not talking about productivity, as in "you have to be productive every day." A day sitting staring at the ocean with your dog is not a wasted day. A day catching up on sleep is not a wasted day. A wasted day, a day where your time and effort are spent doing something that is not serving you in any meaningful way, where you're just biding time, paying your bills until you fucking die — that sucks. And that is what I am done with.

I'm not that person anymore. And I don't want you to be that person either.

I want you to carpe the fucking diem out of this life.

There's nothing stopping you, and don't let your brain or anyone else tell you otherwise. What's holding you back is not lack of money, nor not knowing what to do. It's not a lack of knowledge on how to build a sales funnel or something like that. It's our own selves, our own feelings of worthiness, of confidence, our relationship to risk and fear and failure and judgment and data, and all these deeply human, confusing things that hold us back.

Most people are not naturally built to be who they need to be to be entrepreneurs. Setting aside the Elon Musks of the world who are just naturally entrepreneurial, this stuff runs counter to our biology, to our systemic and societal conditioning — to everything you probably grew up thinking about work.

Most people can and will fit into the Matrix.

You can't. You won't. You don't have to.

This book is meant to be a lighthouse, a guide to finding your way out of the confusion and pain and fear that comes with doing something that requires you to be braver and more resourceful than you ever thought. I hope you'll come back to it again and again, because that means you're growing.

Don't worry about the detours. Your job is to keep finding your way out of the brambles and back onto the path. Be kind to yourself, surround yourself with remarkable people to lean on and learn from, and by god...peel back those layers and show us what you've got.

EPILOGUE

It's all fine and good to read a book like this and feel excited to up your game. It's another thing entirely to *actually up your game*. I've read dozens of books that have me ready to step up and into a better version of me, and a week later I've already forgotten about it.

So while I'm deeply grateful if anything you've read in this book has been helpful or motivating to you, the truth is that I'm in the business of facilitating real, tangible change and transformation.

I want you to feel confident, capable and skilled as a business owner.

I want your company to earn well so that you can be an active participant in creating a more sustainable capitalism.

I want you to feel deeply fulfilled by your work and leave behind a legacy you are insanely proud of.

So please head on over to heatherthorkelson.com to find resources and ways in which we can continue this journey together. As Seth says on the front cover, let's make things better by making better things.

THANK YOU

Writing a first book is a helluva mission and I could never have done it without the support of a handful of stellar humans. So, a big thank you to my first editor Kate Allyson for keeping me on task to get the first draft out of my head. Next-level gratitude to my developmental editor Rachel Allen for guiding me through some intense work over the course of a year to give the content its form and helping me stay the course. Deep bows to my beta readers for such valuable feedback and for helping me see that I had, in fact, created a body of work that matters. Big love to Pernilla, Leela, Lynn, Torill and Sonia for grounding me and making me laugh when I needed it most (aka when I wanted to chuck my laptop in the ocean and run away forever). Mega gratitude to Sutton Long for guiding me through the book design process with such patience and support. And the most massive thanks ever to my husband Rickard for patiently listening to me go off on wild tangents (and secretly hitting the record button on his phone so I wouldn't forget what I said later), as well as always making space for me to write. It really does take a village.

AUTHOR BIO

Heather is a Canadian dual business owner based in rural Sweden. She's spent the majority of her life living abroad since her family moved to Costa Rica when she was 14, which gave her a wanderlust that lasts to this day. After working in corporate throughout her 20's, Heather took the leap into entrepreneurship. She's been a business consultant for incurable entrepreneurs since 2011, helping hundreds of small business owners grow livelihoods that honour their strengths and feed their bank accounts in equal measure. At the same time, she feeds her own entrepreneurial drive through running a polar expedition company that specializes in boutique small ship expeditions in the Arctic and Antarctic. She's excited to share her expertise and experience to support a new wave of values-based entrepreneurs with her first book, *No Plan B*.

Printed in Poland
by Amazon Fulfillment
Poland Sp. z o.o., Wrocław

63309356R00161